Century Makers

Century Makers

One hundred clever things we take for granted which have changed our lives over the last one hundred years

David Hillman & David Gibbs

Welcome Rain
New York

First WELCOME RAIN edition 1999
Published by WELCOME RAIN
New York, New York

First published in Great Britain in 1998
by Weidenfeld & Nicolson
Orion House
5 Upper St Martin's Lane
London WC2H 9EA

Library of Congress information available from
the publisher

ISBN 1-56649-000-6
M 10 9 8 7 6 5 4 3 2 1

Written by David Gibbs
Research by Joanna Jenkins
Designed by David Hillman
and Liza Enebeis
Set in Akzidenz Grotesk and Joanna

Introduction

From the paperclip to Prozac, here are one hundred of the little things we rarely think about but have changed our lives in the 20th century. These are the century makers. Taken with the great pillars of the period – flight, television, nuclear power, computers, space travel and the Internet – they provide the detail in the definition of our times.

The 20th century began in the afterglow of Victorian vigour. Often portrayed as staid and oppressive, the Victorians were hugely inventive and enterprising, enjoying personal liberties that would seem like anarchy today. They gave us electric power, electric light, the telephone, radio, photography, cars, railways – in fact most of the foundations for the gigantic technological and scientific strides that have been taken in the 20th century. They also generated many of the ideas that changed 20th-century thinking, from Darwinism and Communism to the Arts and Crafts Movement.

The spirit of those times was blown away by the First World War. Fought with a strategy of attrition so that the side with the most resources would win, it drained economies and killed 15 million young men in Europe. Suddenly women were needed to be more than nurses and secretaries and they began to fill the gaps, accelerating their release from the assumptions that had governed for so long.

Domestic life changed. Electric power arrived in more and more homes allowing the spread of labour-saving devices such as washing machines, vacuum cleaners and food mixers which had been dreamt up before the war. Social life changed markedly through 1920s and 1930s, and women now had the means to express themselves differently, with new kinds of clothes, hairstyles and make-up.

The brief optimism of the inter-war years died with rise of Fascism and Communism and the Great Depression of the 1930s. After just 21 years of peace the Second World War started. It brought Europe to its knees, straining national resources to breaking point. It did, however, hasten the development of all sorts of inventions: the aerosol, Teflon, the microwave oven and pizza deliveries, while interrupting the progress of others: the electric razor, the ballpoint pen, aluminium foil and nylon stockings. They all joined in to help make the new era of peace that has lasted the rest of the century.

America survived both wars without its economy being crippled, and so became the powerhouse for the peace. Its culture was exported to the world and the idea of youth as something different from childhood or adulthood came into focus, taking its cues largely from Hollywood and American popular music.

Through the latter part of the century, with growth and prosperity the norm for industrialized countries, there has been relative affluence and leisure. Yet life has become faster and our eating, working, shopping and leisure habits have changed immeasurably. Growth and 'the latest thing' have become the watchwords of our time.

Some of our century makers have also unwittingly hindered as well as helped our lives. Aerosol propellant gases damaged the ozone layer until they were changed. Chainsaws have become the means for the destruction of the rainforests. Disposable products clog the environment while, at the other end of the scale, parking meters may generate rage and indignation on city streets.

It is too early to tell whether the new things of the last decade or so are destined to become century makers. Cloning and genetic engineering, the further miniaturization of data processors, mobile phones – these are candidates and are almost certain to be part of the legacy we hand on which will help to make the 21st century.

Contents

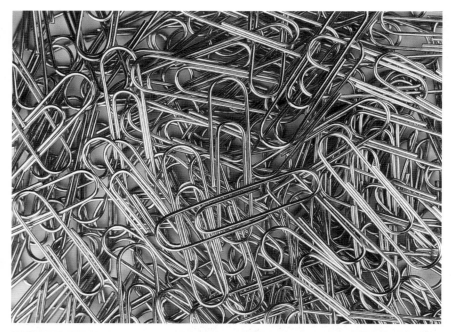

Paperclip

For its sheer usefulness and artful simplicity the paper clip really is one of the great little inventions of the century. Countless billions have been produced since Johann Vaaler, a Norwegian working in Germany, patented the design in 1900.

Vaaler's paper clip is simply a piece of wire, cunningly bent so that the ends do not tear the paper. It has become the standard method of keeping notes, pages and files together in practically every office and home in the world. In 1989 Norway recognized its inventor's achievement by raising a giant paper clip in his honour near Oslo.

Safety razor

In 1901 King Camp Gillette patented his idea for a safety razor designed to be used with disposable blades. Production began in 1903, but by the end of the year Gillette had sold just 51 safety razors and 168 blades. The invention had all the signs of being a big flop. It was with some relief to Gillette that in the following year 90,000 safety razors were sold in the USA. The idea had caught on and by the late 1940s, when electric razors were beginning to have an impact on the market, 16 million safety razors were being sold a year, with production of blades at around 27 million a week.

Gillette stood before his shaving mirror in 1895 and thought just how little of his cut-throat razor was being used in the actual process of shaving. Most of the fine steel in the blade was doing nothing but supporting the edge. He wondered about producing a razor blade that was practically all edge and little else.

What was also in Gillette's mind was a comment made some time earlier by his employer, who had urged him to find something that people would use only once and then throw away – the concept of the disposable. If Gillette could make his thin, flat blade disposable, and house it in a device that would make it hard for the shaver to cut himself, he was convinced he would be on to a winner.

Steel manufacturers told him that a blade that was thin enough, flat enough and sharp enough was 'impossible' – a word that has deterred few inventors. Gillette formed the American Safety Razor Company on 28 September 1901 and the problem of the thin, flat, sharp blade was finally solved by his sole employee, an engineer named William Nickerson.

Once the idea of throw-away blades had been established, someone had to come up with long-life blades that would give more than one shave. This duly happened in 1956, when the British firm Wilkinson Sword began to market its stainless-steel blades, a lead soon followed by Gillette. The two have been leap-frogging each other with innovations ever since.

The Marilyn Monroe look-alike shaving on the cover of Esquire magazine in 1965 was for an article on the masculinization of the American woman, a slant on the women's lib movement. The art director was George Lois, working in collaboration with photographer Carl Fischer. Esquire started life as a trade magazine for men's clothes in 1933. During the 1940s and 1950s it established itself as the first popular magazine devoted mainly to men's interests, covering politics, fashion, health, the arts — and women. One of Esquire's famous attractions were the *Varga* and *Petty Girls*, and it is said that they were handed on to a certain journalist working on the magazine named Hugh Hefner, who went away and started Playboy in 1953.

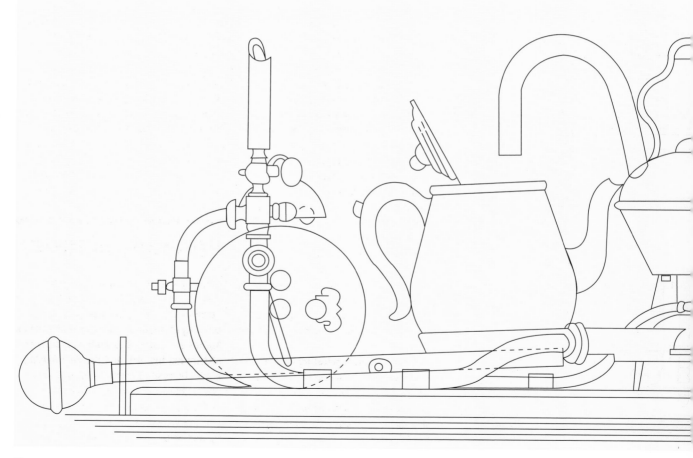

Tea-maker

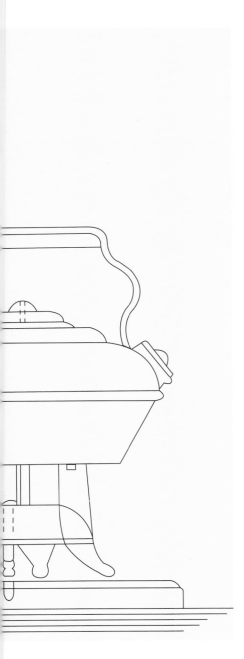

Having freshly brewed tea waiting when you wake up is some people's idea of heaven. Although various ingenious contraptions had been devised to achieve this towards the end of the last century, it was Frank Clarke, a Birmingham gunsmith, who demonstrated the first working automatic tea-maker in 1902. Clarke's machine was controlled by a clock with an alarm set to the time tea was required. Before the alarm went off, a kettle with a moving plate was heated by methylated spirits, which had been lit by a striker moving across the head of a match. When the kettle boiled the moving plate inside it shook, activating a tipping mechanism that poured the water into the teapot. As the alarm bell sounded the striker plate moved over the burning meths to extinguish it.

Despite the attempts of Clark and others, the first tea-making machine that the British really took to was invented in 1936 by Brenner Thornton. His design eliminated the precarious balancing acts and dangers of earlier devices. A special electric kettle was timed to boil minutes before the alarm

Taken from a Victorian patent for an early tea-making machine, with alarm clock, burner, kettle and teapot. The precarious arrangement was meant to light itself, boil the water, tip it on to the tea and then wake up the sleeper, if it hadn't already.

was due to go off. The boiling water was automatically decanted directly on to the tea in a pot and the kettle was switched off. The weight of water in the pot also triggered the switch of an integral bedside lamp. So the sleeper awoke with the bedside lamp on, the alarm ringing — and freshly brewed tea waiting to be poured.

The rights to Thornton's design were bought by Goblin, who introduced the Teasmade in 1937. Wary of the machine at first, the British gradually took to it. Today throughout the country — in hotels, in Bed-and-Breakfast accommodation and in over two million homes — Teasmades satisfy the British nation's almost obsessive insistence on a cup of tea first thing in the morning. The machine has been restyled and offered in a huge variety of different colours over the years, but the basic mechanism, which does make good tea, has stayed the same.

Vacuum cleaner

Hubert Cecil Booth, a bridge engineer, was appalled when he saw clouds of dust being thrown up by the compressed-air cleaning of a railway carriage at St Pancras Station in London. The method merely redistributed the dirt, and the dust settled again. Instead of trying to blow it away, Booth thought of sucking it up into a receptacle. A prototype machine was made and the Vacuum Cleaner Company was formed on 25 February 1902.

Right: *Peter Sellers as Inspector Clouseau in* **The Return of the Pink Panther** *created mayhem with a vacuum cleaner in one of the film's brilliantly timed set pieces. Directed by Blake Edwards in 1974, it was the fourth Pink Panther film and also starred Catherine Schell, Christopher Plummer and Herbert Lom.*

Booth's machines were initially used only by his company to provide a cleaning service. There was little or no electricity in houses at the time, and so a Booth vacuum pump mounted on a cart turned up outside a customer's house with a hose long enough to reach any part of the dwelling. This was fed through a window and the suction cleaning was begun. The racket made by the pump in the street frequently frightened passing horses, leading to a number of law suits. It took a ruling by the Lord Chief Justice to uphold Booth's right to operate his machines in the street.

During preparations for the coronation of King Edward VII in 1902,

the carpets under the twin thrones in Westminster Abbey were discovered at the last minute to be filthy. It was Vacuum Cleaner Company machines that came to the rescue. The king heard of the marvellous cleaners and ordered two – one for Buckingham Palace and one for Windsor Castle. This royal patronage assured the future of the vacuum cleaner and soon everybody who was anybody wanted the service, which was even provided on some occasions as an entertainment at soirées. Booth's Vacuum Cleaner Company eventually became Goblin, which continues to manufacture vacuum cleaners along with a range of other electrical household goods.

The first portable electric vacuum cleaner was introduced in San Francisco by Chapman & Skinner in 1905. The following year a similar machine was produced by the Vacuum Cleaner Company in London. In 1907 W. H. Hoover, a harness maker of New Berlin (now called Canton), Ohio, saw a remarkable hand-built upright vacuum cleaner with a dust bag made out of a pillowcase attached to a handle made out of a broom. It had been put together by J. Murray Spangler, a janitor in a New Berlin department store.

Hoover bought the rights and produced his first commercial model in 1907. Within three years he had expanded production and opened a factory in Canada from where his Suction Sweeper Company began to export vacuum cleaners to the Old World in 1912. So popular were the company's models that 'Hoover' became the generic name for the vacuum cleaner for the best part of the century.

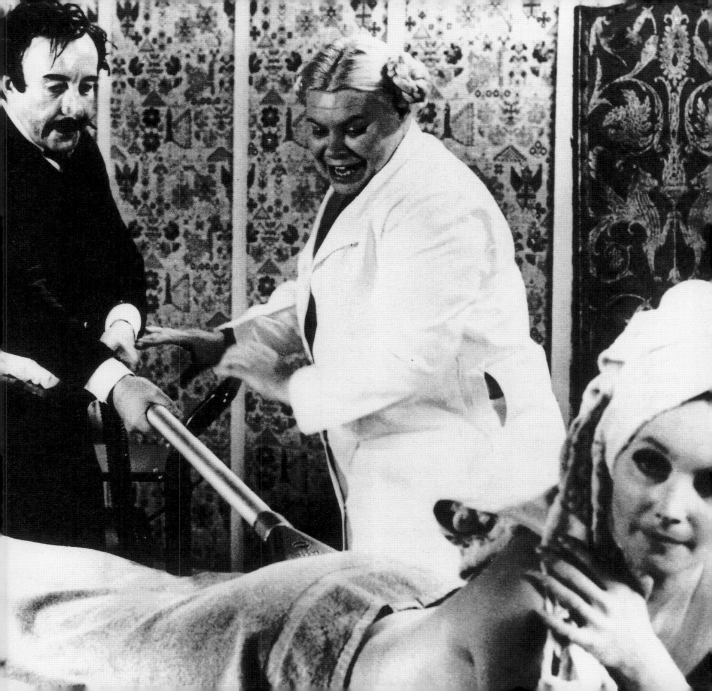

Elvis Presley's 'Teddy Bear', taken from his second film, Loving You, reached number one in 1957, and fans inundated him with thousands and thousands of teddy bears. Presley had been the revolutionary originator of Memphis rockabilly with his early recordings for the Sun label in 1954 and 1955. Moving to RCA in 1956 he recorded an unprecedented string of extraordinary hits, starting with 'Heartbreak Hotel' and including 'Hound Dog', 'All Shook Up' and 'Jailhouse Rock'. His on-stage persona was as radical and controversial as his music and caused much consternation in conservative America. In 1958 he was drafted into the army and it was as though another person returned in 1960. Although Presley assumed his crown as 'The King' by virtue of those five years in the 1950s, his later career was blighted by a series of second-rate films and gross, sweaty displays of overblown sentimentality on stage. He died in 1977.

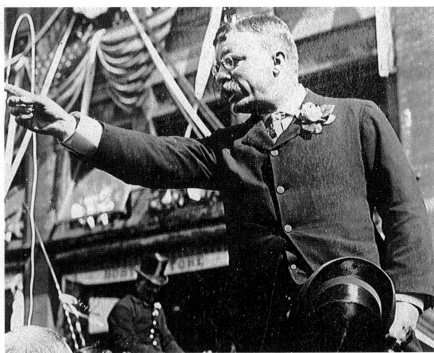

President Theodore 'Teddy' Roosevelt, inspiration for the teddy bear, speaking in 1902 at Willimantic, Connecticut.

Teddy bear

There are two claims to the invention of the cuddly, dumpy toy bears called teddy bears – one from a Russian immigrant in New York and one from a German family firm in the Black Forest. The 'teddy bear' name certainly first appeared in a US trade magazine called *Playthings* in 1906, and was thoroughly approved of by President Theodore 'Teddy' Roosevelt, with whom it was associated. Teddies became all the rage in the years leading up to the First World War, and have been favourite mascots and part of family life ever since.

In November 1902 President Roosevelt took time off to go on a bear-hunting trip in Mississippi. After several days and no bears, his hosts made one final effort to find something for the President to shoot, and managed to flush out a grizzly bear-cub from the woods. They drove it towards the President's party, but Roosevelt famously refused to shoot the little thing.

A cartoon by Clifford K. Berryman of the incident appeared soon after in the *Washington Post* and was syndicated to other papers. This was seen by Morris Mitchtom, proprietor of a novelty shop in Brooklyn, New York. Spotting an opportunity, he asked his wife to make a toy bear from stuffed brown plush with moveable limbs and buttons for eyes. He then displayed what he called 'Teddy's Bear' alongside Berryman's cartoon in his window. The following year he formed the Ideal Novelty and Toy Co. and was soon manufacturing the bears by the hundred.

Meanwhile Richard Steiff, whose family firm made toys in Germany, also had the idea of making a toy bear with moveable limbs and a moveable head after seeing bears at Stuttgart Zoo. The Steiff bear was shown at the 1903 Leipzig Toy Fair, where it landed an order for 3,000 bears from an American buyer. By 1907 annual production in Germany had reached 974,000. At a rally at Philadelphia Zoo in 1982 marking the 80th anniversary of the teddy bear, the managing director of Steiff turned up with the 1902 prototype bear chained to his waist.

Vacuum flask

Although the Scottish scientist Sir James Dewar first came up with the idea of a double-walled glass vacuum vessel for keeping liquids hot or cold, it was a German student of his, Rheinhold Burger, who turned it into a practical product. He became a partner in the Munich firm of Burger und Aschenbrenner, which

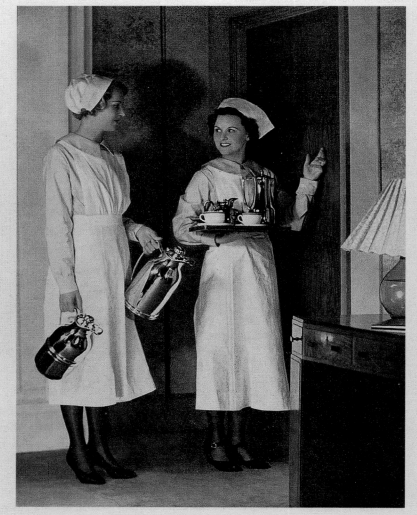

Memo. to Staff: Prepare coffee, hot water, shaving water at 7.30 a.m. Place in Thermos Jugs for service when wanted.

Memo. to Guests: Ring for coffee when you wake. If you fall asleep again, it won't matter. The Thermos Jugs will keep it piping hot.

Memo. for Christmas: Thermos Jugs for every body

THERMOS
REGD. TRADE MARK

THERMOS (1925) LIMITED
Seymour Road, London, E.10

first began producing the vacuum flask in 1904. They couldn't decide what to call the new type of container, so a public competition was held to find a name. A local resident came up with 'Thermos', the Greek for 'heat'.

Thermos GmbH was founded later in 1904, and the British rights were acquired by A. E. Gutmann in 1905. These were taken over in turn by Thermos Ltd, which was set up in London in 1907. Thermos flasks were expensive to begin with, as their glass innards had to be hand blown. But in 1911 Thermos Ltd mechanized production, which halved the price. While the Thermos flask was primarily meant for use away from the house, Thermos jugs also became popular domestically; they were originally advertised as a method of keeping tea and coffee warm. Britain became the main centre for production, and vacuum flasks were exported worldwide.

Like many innovative products of the century, the fortunes of the Thermos were affected by the demands of war. In the First World War a Zeppelin bombed the Thermos factory in Tottenham. During the Second World War production was dedicated to the Services, and it was reckoned that every time 1,000 Allied bombers went out on a raid, between 10,000 and 12,000 Thermos flasks went with them.

A guileless magazine advertisement in 1938 promoting the benefits of the Thermos jug. Domestic servants were a feature in the lives of the better-off until the Second World War.

The American hamburger has become the universal food, transcending local culture, language, politics and traditional cuisine.

Hamburger

Despite its obviously German name, the beef patty in a bun is an American invention and was first officially recorded at the Louisiana Purchase Exhibition in St Louis, Missouri in 1904. It has since become the prime universal food, supplementing if not supplanting national eating habits and regional culinary traditions developed over centuries. More than food, the hamburger is a symbol and conveyer of American popular culture in a world where marketing communications have become such a dominant influence.

There are three strands to the story that led to the hamburger in the bun, which took over and redefined American eating habits. German immigrants settling around Cincinnati originally brought over the finely chopped beef of Hamburg, which they browned on the outside and left very rare inside. The British and Irish had another tradition, called the Salisbury Steak, which was also made of chopped beef and was well cooked all the way through. With these two established it took the sandwich idea to complete the picture. (This was attributed in the 18th century to John Montagu, Fourth Earl of Sandwich, a gambler who placed his meat course between two slices of bread so that he could stay at the tables while eating.)

The hamburger as we know it became a firmly established favourite in America during the early part of the century. After the Second World War the rise of youth culture and the youth market sent hamburgers into orbit. Caring less about social meals at the family table and what their mothers called 'eating properly', kids took their new disposable income and spent it on hamburgers and Coke.

A company called McDonald's later spotted that in three out of four families it is the children who decide where to eat. Richard and Maurice McDonald opened the first McDonald's in San Bernardino, California in 1948. In 1954 they granted Ray Kroc exclusive franchise rights in the USA and he opened his first McDonald's on 15 April 1955 in Des Plaines, Illinois. With an unerringly consistent product and a well-run franchise operation, McDonald's led the global spread of the eat-where-you-are hamburger habit. Promotional links with Hollywood, electronic entertainment giants and American sports helped McDonald's ride the primacy of American popular culture. By the end of the 1990s McDonald's were operating in 109 countries with 23,000 restaurants, including 29 in Hamburg.

Swedish-born Claes Oldenburg became one of the leaders of American Pop art with his giant sculptures of food. Floor Hamburger was created in 1962 out of canvas stuffed with foam rubber. It is now in the Art Gallery of Ontario, Toronto. Gaining American citizenship in the early 1950s, Oldenburg became involved in the revolt against Abstract Expressionism and took part in the 'Happenings' of the late 1950s. He turned from painting to three-dimensional work, inspired by the street life of New York. In 1961 he opened The Store, where he sold his sculptural replicas of domestic objects. Later sculptures include the giant lipstick at Yale University in 1969 and the 60 ft (20 m) Match Cover erected in Barcelona in 1992.

Washing Machine was painted in 1961 by Roy Lichtenstein, who became famous in the 1960s for his large-scale Pop art images inspired by comic strips. Among the best known is the heroic American fighter pilot in action entitled Whaam!, 1963, which is now in the Tate Gallery. Lichtenstein is said to have adopted this style after one of his children, who was reading a comic book, said, 'I bet you can't paint as good as that.' In the mid-1960s he began making Pop versions of modern masterpieces, and later commissions included public works such as Mural with Blue Brushstrokes for the Equitable Building, New York, in 1986. Lichtenstein died at the age of 74 in 1997.

Electric washing machine

After the washboard, mangle and dolly of the last century, there were many more attempts to provide further mechanical assistance to the chore of washing – some gas-powered, some using steam, none particularly effective. Then as more and more American homes were connected up to electricity in the early years of the century, all sorts of new domestic gadgets became possible. In 1907 the American engineer Alva J. Fisher designed the Thor, the world's first electric washing machine, which was made by the Hurley Machine Corporation of Chicago.

By the 1920s washing machines were beginning to have a big impact on domestic life in the USA. Meanwhile Britain and continental Europe were a little behind in domestic electrification, and washing machines remained a luxury. In the Harrods catalogue of 1929 one model that was advertised could also take attachments to mince meat, make ice cream, sausages and butter – even clean knives.

In 1957 the twin tub arrived – a top-loading machine with one tub for washing and the other for spinning. The first automatic washing machines appeared in the 1960s, and by the 1990s they were available with all sorts of programmes and temperatures, some also combining driers, controlled by microprocessors.

WOI

In the 18th century,
when logic and science were the fashion,

men

tried to talk like men.
The 20th century has reversed
the process.

Aldous Huxley

The famous Persil advertising proposition, which has been a feature of the brand's promotion for over half a century, plays on the pride of a mother in the superiority of her family's whites. The opener: 'Someone's Mum doesn't know...' led to the pay-off: 'what someone's Mum ought to know. That Persil washes whiter.' After a while the copyline became so familiar that the second half went without saying.

Washing powder

In 1907 Persil was launched as the first washing powder by Henkel & Cie in Dusseldorf, Germany. The name was derived from two of its active ingredients: perborate and silicate. Two years later Persil was acquired by the British company Joseph Crosfield of Warrington, Cheshire, but it was not until after the First World War, when Lever Brothers took over the reins, that Persil sales began to soar. It has been one of the leading brand names ever since.

Washing powder's rise required two things: change in social attitudes and the introduction of machines for washing. Domestic drudgery became less of a virtue after the First World War, and with female emancipation (which grew into women's lib in the 1960s and, not quite so profoundly, girl-power in the 1990s) women began to demand that less time be spent doing household chores. By the 1920s the electric washing machine had arrived to help. Since then washing powder advertising and promotion aimed at the 'housewife' has been notoriously cut-throat.

The first washing powders were derived from soap, but it is detergents that have now become the world's prime cleaning agents. These are made from fats and sulphuric acid and have a structure similar to that of soap molecules. However, detergents have the advantage in that they are cheaper to produce and do not produce a scum in harder waters. Early detergents were developed from coal tar in Germany during the First World War but after the Second Word War synthetic organic detergents came increasingly into use.

Modern detergents with alkyl benzene as their main base were introduced in the 1950s. Since then all sorts of other additives have been made for enhancing specific performances. Enzymes, which are biological catalysts produced in living cells, began to be added in the 1960s to make 'biological' detergents, which remove body stains better. The newer 'green' detergents have no bleaches or phosphates, which are the causes of the effluent foam in rivers.

Paper cup/ Dixie cup

At the turn of the century most public buildings and transport stations in the USA offered free drinking water which was dispensed from a communal tin cup. It occurred to Hugh Moore, a Harvard University drop-out from Kansas, that this was a highly unsanitary practice. He had an idea for a water cooler that came with its own disposable paper cups. With fellow Kansan Lawrence Luellan he established the American Water Supply Co. of New England in 1908, and they secured considerable backing for the idea from the American Can Co. They formed the Public Cup Vendor Co. in 1909.

On evidence that was accumulating on disease caused by germs on public drinking cups, in 1909 the Kansas State Health Officer ordered that shared drinking cups be banned from public places – and that included all railway trains which passed though the state. The oppotunity was not lost on Moore and Luellan, and the Lackawanna Railroad was the first of many to switch to their cups.

The company name was changed again to the Individual Drinking Cup Company in 1910, and in 1912 its sole product became known as the Health Kup. Finally in 1919 the name of Dixie Cup was adopted, and from 1921, as ice cream also opened up as a big market for its products, the company grew fast.

During the Second World War the American Armed Forces, hospitals, the American Red Cross and factory cafeterias across the country all switched to disposable paper cups. Dixie Cup entered the consumer market for the first time after the war with five-cup kitchen dispensers. In 1957 fate took the company full circle when it was acquired by the American Can Co., the original backers of the venture in 1908. The Dixie brand changed hands once more in 1982 when it was bought by what *Forbes* magazine called 'the best little paper company in America', the James River Corporation.

When you don't have any use for it any more, discard it. That may be all right if it's a disposable paper cup, but not if it's a person.

HEL
BO

THE ONE AND
Wonder

THE ORIGINAL PUSH-UP PLUNGE BRA.

Eva Herzigova in the Wonderbra poster caused a stir in the 1990s and signified how much attitudes to undergarments had changed over the century. The advertising campaign, which started in the UK, was translated to other countries and the state of undress modified according to the local sensibilities – to the point where in the Middle East, the model wore a jumper, destroying the point.

Bra

'A brassière for dressy occasions' was mentioned in American *Vogue* in 1909 and as 'a necessity for those of generous build' in 1912 by *Queen* magazine in Britain. However, it was Mary Phelps Jacob, later Caresse Crosby, who filed a patent for the brassière in 1914. Mary

LO
YS.

LE IN SIZES 32-38 ABC.

Phelps's first effort was a pair of hand-kerchiefs, a length of pink ribbon and thread to stitch them together – simply made to free herself from the grip of the corset. Her patent landed her a contract for $15,000 by Warner Brothers Corset Co., reckoned since to be worth in the order of $20 million.

It was the revival of the empire line by designer Paul Poiret in 1908 that was the beginning of the end of the fashion for the tortuous and unnatural shape that could only be sustained by the corset.

Although Poiret's simpler clothes were a declaration of war on the corset, it did not disappear but was instead lowered around the hips and thighs, releasing the waist – and necessitating a brassière. By the end of the First World War the artificial constriction of women by their clothes was finally coming to an end – or so it was said. Ironically, the bra was used as a flattening garment in the 1920s fashion for the waistless and breastless look that focused on the legs. After 1930 the bra began to be used to delineate the breast and moulded rubber pads, or 'falsies', became available for inserting into the bra if your shape or size was not quite fashionable.

The end of the Second World War and the reaction against austerity brought the New Look and saw all underwear, bra included, becoming more decorative, with added flouncing, ruching and lace. In the days of the 1950s sweater girls, especially in Britain, the jumper was filled out by high-flying brassières wired and boned to maximize every last inch of nature's endowment. Foam rubber and oil-filled falsies were also used.

The 1960s saw the arrival of the 'no-bra' bra to suit the soft, body-conscious clothes of the decade. By then the bra had become much more than a mere item of clothing. It was not only a symbol of sexuality but, like the corset before it, a garment that some thought also signified repression and subservience to men. It was thus an

Defiant bra burning became a symbolic demonstration of women's liberation during the 1960s. The seriousness of the gesture was diluted by the guffaws of the press, and this girl is burning her bra purely as a publicity stunt.

obvious target for the new wave of vociferous women's liberationists who gained some notoriety by burning their bras in public.

During the 1970s, the prevalent feminism made for an uneasy relationship between women and their bras. But in the 1980s and 1990s the bra as a positive symbol of sexuality returned and was marketed with a new boldness and humour not possible in the coyness of the earlier part of the century. The bra had supported and survived many fashions – ultimately changing from being an intimate to an explicit, indeed exhibitionist, garment.

Neon lighting

Neon lighting was displayed for the
first time at the Paris Motor Show on
3 December 1910. It consisted of two
tubes 1¾ inches (4.5 cm) in diameter and
115 feet (35 m) long, which illuminated
the peristyle of the Grand Palais, where the
exhibition was held. The lighting had been
developed by the French physicist Georges
Claude, who discovered that passing electrical current through inert gases in vacuum
tubes produced coloured light. Neon lighting is highly efficient and generates hardly
any heat. Today, the glass tubes can be
tinted with numerous phosphorescent pig-
ments and can last for up to 30 years.

Georges Claude had envisaged that his
invention would be used for ordinary
lighting, but at this early stage only a
red glow was possible. An advertising
man, Jacques Fonesque, persuaded him
to concentrate on illuminated signs
and the rights were acquired by
Fonesque's agency, Paz et Silva. In 1912
a sign announcing 'Le Palace Coiffure'
was erected over a barber shop in
Montmartre. The first neon advertising
sign was the word 'Cinzano', on the
front of 72, boulevard Haussmann.

By 1914 Paris had 150 neon signs
and their popularity spread around
the world. In the 1930s Times Square
in New York and Piccadilly Circus in
London had become famous for their
displays of neon advertising. In 1946
neon hit Las Vegas, which took to it
as if it were its own.

30

In 1935 President Roosevelt went to the Arizona/Nevada border and opened the gigantic Boulder (later Hoover) Dam on the Colorado River. Designed as part of the 'New Deal' to make the desert bloom, it also had the unforeseen effect of transforming in ten years the dusty little desert town of Las Vegas into the neon-lit capital of American pleasures. Now at night it is lit up by a swirling forest of multi-coloured lights, one of the modern wonders of the world. Just one of the big downtown hotels uses as much electricity as the houses in a town of 60,000 people. Binion's Horseshoe Casino claims to have the world's largest individual display, with no less than eight miles (13 km) of neon tubing.

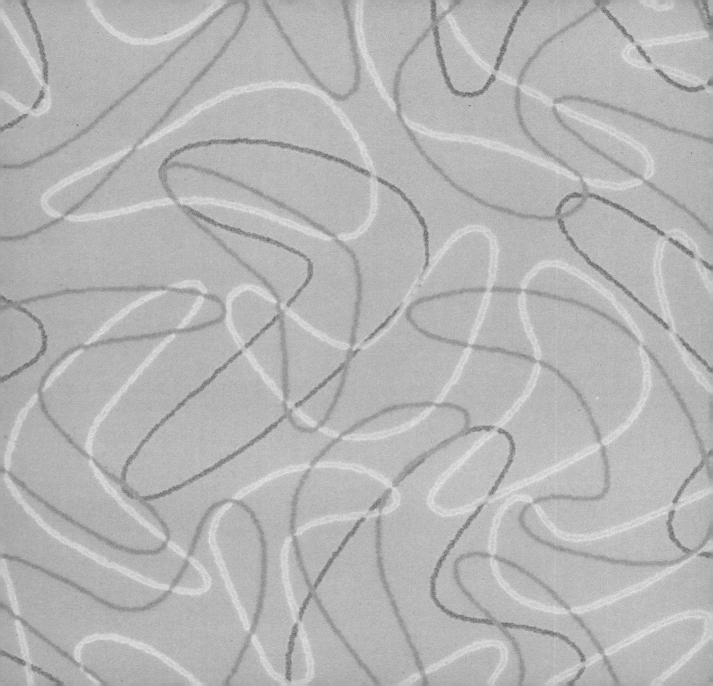

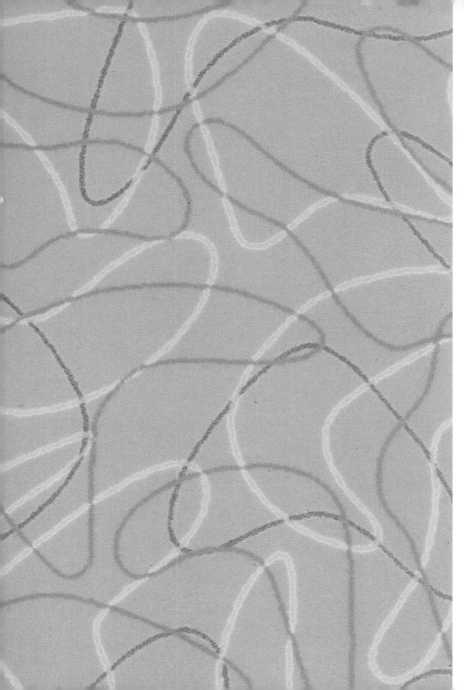

Formica

Dr Leo Baekeland, who also invented Bakelite, took out the first laminate patent in 1911 and, working with two young engineers from the Westinghouse Corporation, developed a paper-based laminate for use as electrical insulation. Dr Baekeland's collaborators were Herbert A. Faber and Daniel J. O'Conor, who went on to found the Formica Corporation in 1913. Formica was so named because the new material was a substitute 'for mica', the mineral widely used at the time for electrical insulation.

It was not until the mid-1920s that the Formica Corporation had the idea of producing laminates for furniture. Designers and manufacturers immediately took to this new 'modern' material. The laminated surface is typically about $\frac{1}{16}$ of an inch (1.5 mm) thick and is made by impregnating several layers of unrefined 'kraft' paper with phenolic acid and compressing the sheets between heated plates of polished

Raymond Loewy was hired by Formica in 1957 to exploit the graphic design possibilities of the laminate and he produced these characteristic shapes and colours of the times. In a career that spanned five decades, from the 1930s to the 1970s, Loewy's best-known designs include the Coca-Cola bottle, the Lucky Strike cigarette packet and Pepsodent toothpaste packaging, Studebaker cars and Greyhound buses, the streamlined Pennsylvania Railroad S-1 locomotive and the interior of NASA's Skylab.

steel. The resulting sheet is then bonded to wood, chipboard or plywood.

Until 1925 all laminates were either brown or black, but in 1927 Formica patented a method for decorating the laminate by lithographing the top layer. The first patterns were imitation wood-grains and marble effects, and it quickly became popular for use in restaurants, bars and soda fountains. Shiny black laminates remained the choice of designers working in the Modern Style during the 1930s; for example, Donald Deskey combined black laminate with chrome and aluminium in his famous designs for New York's Radio City Music Hall. In 1937 melamine began to be used to impregnate the top layer of the laminate so as to increase its hardness and water resistance. It also made it easier to produce lighter colours for the surface.

In 1957 Formica hired Raymond Loewy to create new decorative patterns and colours lines and he came up with the characteristic 'atomic' black and pastel boomerang shapes on white fields that became so associated with the style of the times, especially in kitchens. Laminated wood-grain effects continued to be the popular choice for other rooms in the house and Formica even produced a laminate with a real wood veneer impregnated with melamine.

New York's art deco Radio City Music Hall, part of the Rockefeller Center, built in 1932, included furniture in black shiny Formica combined with chrome, steel and aluminium, designed by Donald Deskey.

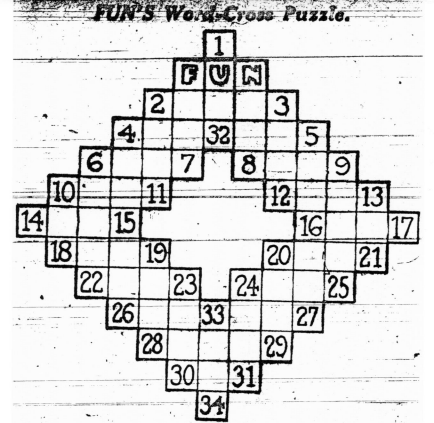

FUN'S Word-Cross Puzzle.

Crossword

A new game was introduced to readers of the *New York World* on 21 December 1913. It had been created by Arthur Wynne, who was employed in the newspaper's 'tricks and jokes department'. Wynne was from Liverpool and had the idea from a Victorian parlour game that his grandfather used to play, called Magic Squares.

The clues to early puzzles were not difficult, being mainly word definitions – as are still found in American crosswords and British 'quick' crosswords. Peculiar to Britain is the cryptic crossword puzzle, an invention that first appeared in the *Saturday Westminster* in 1925. The originator is known only by his pseudonym 'Toquemada', a reference to the Inquisitor General of the Spanish Inquisition, notorious for devising particular tortures. Whoever the 20th-century Toquemada was, he invented the cryptic clue that contains all sorts of cunning snares: puns, anagrams, literary allusions and even cricket terms.

This style was adopted by *The Times* when its first crossword appeared on 1 February 1930, compiled by Adrian Bell. To meet the highbrow affectations of its readers *The Times* crossword appeared for a while in Latin and Greek as well as English.

The first ever crossword was based on simple definitions and synonyms.

FILL in the small squares with words which agree with the following definitions:

2—3. What bargain hunters enjoy.

4—5. A written acknowledgment.

6—7. Such and nothing more.

10—11. A bird.

14—15. Opposed to less.

18—19. What this puzzle is.

22—23. An animal of prey.

26—27. The close of a day.

28—29. To elude.

30—31. The plural of is.

8—9. To cultivate.

12—13. A bar of wood or iron.

16—17. What artists learn to do.

20—21. Fastened.

24—25. Found on the seashore.

10—18. The fibre of the gomuti palm.

6—22. What we all should be.

4—26. A day dream.

2—11. A talon.

19—28. A pigeon.

F—7. Part of your head.

23—30. A river in Russia.

1—32. To govern.

33—34. An aromatic plant.

N—8. A fist.

24—31. To agree with.

3—12. Part of a ship.

20—29. One.

5—27. Exchanging.

9—25. To sink in mud.

13—21. A boy.

35

In 1964 a Pop art show opened at the Stable Gallery in New York featuring a room full of oversized replicas of cartons including Del Monte peaches, Campbell's tomato juice, Heinz tomato ketchup – and Brillo soap pads. Reminiscing about the 1960s art scene, Pop artist Robert Indiana said: 'The most striking opening of that period was definitely Andy's "Brillo Box" show'. Andy was of course Andy Warhol, the most famous figure in American Pop art. The screenprints he turned out in his studio, The Factory, in the early 1960s included his characteristic repeated images and famous renditions of Marilyn Monroe, Elvis Presley and Elizabeth Taylor. Later, he broadened his activity into 'underground' films, including the six-hour-long Sleep of somebody doing just that, and managing the rock group The Velvet Underground. Cultivating a deliberately bland persona he ensured he was constantly in the eye of society. Often derided for being more concerned with publicity than art, the appeal of his prints and paintings with their imagery, colour and visual rhythm nevertheless endures. Warhol died in 1987 leaving $100 million, most of which went to set up the Andy Warhol foundation.

Brillo pad

The steel-wool pad with special red soap called Brillo was invented to clean the new aluminium pots and pans that were coming on to the market at the turn of the century. The product was patented and the name registered as a trademark in 1913. A company lawyer, Milton B. Loeb, came up with the name and went on to become the majority shareholder, working with the brand until his death in 1972.

A New York door-to-door salesman called Mr Brady was travelling around New England in the early 1900s selling the new aluminium pots and pans (see Aluminium foil, page 116). After complaints about how difficult it was to clean his utensils Brady turned to his brother-in-law, Mr Ludwig, who was a manufacturer of costume jewellery. He had the idea of combining

the scouring and polishing properties of steel wool with a special soap containing jeweller's rouge.

Brady soon found that the new cleaning concoction was outselling his pots and pans, and with Ludwig he approached the lawyer Milton B. Loeb to help form a company to manufacture and market the product. Loeb did more than provide professional advice and services. Having named the product (which he is said to have derived from the Latin *beryllus*, which means shine), he went on to become treasurer and then president of the Brillo Manufacturing Co. Loeb remained president of the company until it was sold to the Purex Corporation in 1963, when he went to oversee its British operations.

Brillo produced the special cakes of red soap plus wads of steel wool that were the original Brillo pads in its factory in Brooklyn. They were sold at first by salesmen like Brady, but when F. W. Woolworth started to carry the line in 1918, followed by grocery stores all over the country, Brillo's success was assured.

The product remained largely unchanged until 1930 when Brillo introduced its steel-wool pads impregnated with the soap. After the war Brillo became the world's best-selling steel-wool cleaner – although it was later overtaken by its arch rival SOS, which was formed on the West Coast only a few years after Brillo. Since 1969, Brillo's two main factories have both been in London – London, Ohio and London, England.

Stainless steel

From the Iron Age through the Industrial Revolution to the present day, corrosion has always been the trouble with the basic material of industrial society. The search for a steel that did not suffer from this drawback ended on 20 August 1913, when Harry Brearley, head of the Brown Firth research laboratories in the Sheffield cutlery industry, came up with a steel containing 12.8 per cent chromium and 0.24 per cent carbon. It was stainless. Brearley's discovery was inspired by a visit he had made to the Royal Small Arms factory in Enfield to discuss the failure of gun barrels owing to internal corrosion. Although his new steel turned out to be unsuitable for guns, he knew that its hardness and resistance to corrosion would give it a future in pistons, valves, spindles – and cutlery.

The first use of stainless steel was for aircraft engine valves in the First World War. In 1919, after some resistance from conservatives in the cutlery industry and disagreement between Brearley and Firth's about patents, Sheffield cutlers started production of stainless-steel cutlery, surgical scalpels and tools.

New York's Chrysler Building was clad in stainless steel in 1930. In 1934 the *Queen Mary* was launched bristling with stainless steel fittings. The Second World War saw the extensive use of stainless steel in aircraft engines, including Frank Whittle's first jet

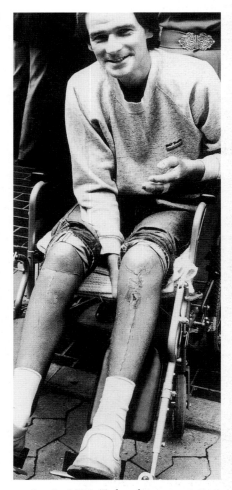

engine in 1941. Today there are over 200 types of stainless steel, containing chromium, nickel and other alloying elements. Their uses are countless, including the internal workings of parking meters, advanced aerospace systems, the whole of the Lloyd's of London building, cutlery and the kitchen sink.

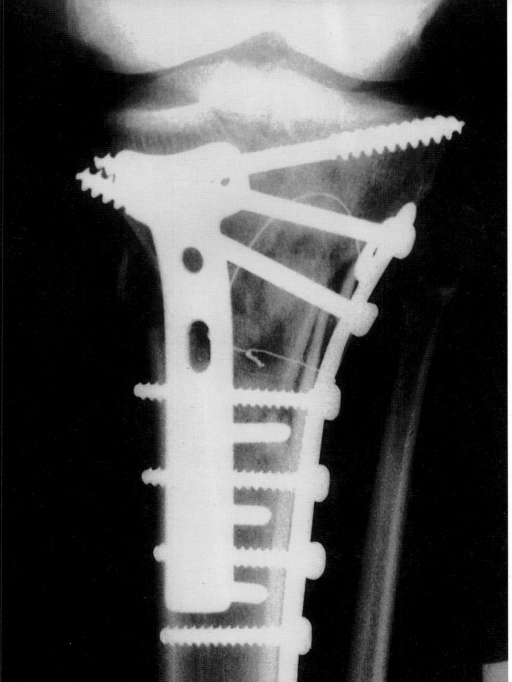

Barry Sheene, World 500 cc Motorcycle Champion in 1976 and 1977, was involved in a bone-shattering crash at high speed while practising on his Yamaha 500 for the Silverstone Grand Prix in 1982. Surgeon Nigel Cobb operated on both legs and wrist at St Matthew's Hospital in Northampton using stainless-steel splints, braces and screws made by AO in Switzerland. Each piece of metal had to be exactly the same type, otherwise the electrolytic effect would cause the bone to disintegrate. Sheene recovered, carried on racing and now lives in Australia, working as a commentator.

Zip/zipper

Although the idea for an interlocking fastener was patented in 1893 by the Chicago engineer Whitcomb Judson, the zip as we know it was invented by Gideon Sundback, a Swede working in America, and patented in 1913. His design had two tapes sewn on to the edges of the garment to be opened or closed. Each tape carried fine metal teeth which interlocked when closed by a sliding clip. A similar design was patented in Europe by Catherina Kuhn-Moos.

The use of zips had its first boost with the First World War when in 1917 the US Navy equipped its pilots with windproof flying suits that were snugly and tightly closed with slide fasteners. The US Army and the Air Corps also adopted them. After the war it was ex-servicemen who began to spread the 'zipper' habit, which had yet to catch on for civilian clothes. The 'zipper' name was actually coined in 1923 by B. G. Work of B. F. Goodrich Co. to describe the slide fasteners that were used in a new design of overshoes from the company.

After zip-fasteners were introduced for clothing in the USA in the 1920s, they quickly gained widespread acceptance for many uses and in 1927

The Rolling Stones 1971 Sticky Fingers album cover, designed by Andy Warhol, was provocatively adorned with a real zip on Mick Jagger's jeans.

sports suits became the first clothing to be fitted with zips in Britain. The first couturier to use the fasteners on women's dresses was Mme Schiaparelli at her Paris fashion house in 1930. In 1934 the Prince of Wales, the Duke of York and Lord Mountbatten asked their tailors to put zips in their trousers for the flies, and from 1935 the zip began to be a common feature in men's clothing.

Traffic lights

Cleveland, Ohio is credited with installing the first true traffic lights in 1914. Manually operated lights were introduced in New York in 1918. The idea crossed the Atlantic and the first traffic lights were installed in Leeds in 1923, coming to London in 1925. By the 1990s traffic lights, coordinated by a central control using camera surveillance and computers, were still keeping the traffic moving in vehicle-saturated cities.

The first road traffic signals were derived from the railways. A Mr Knight, superintendent of the South-Eastern Railway in England, thought up the first traffic signal, which was put up in London on Bridge Street, Westminster, in 1868. It was a cast-iron lamp post combined with a railway-type semaphore signal operated by a policeman. A light was also installed to control vehicles entering the Houses of Parliament, but it exploded.

By 1918, congestion on Fifth Avenue in New York City had become too much for the policemen on point duty to handle. So the city decided to control the traffic by using a system of coloured lights. A series of signal towers were placed down the centre of the street, each with a red, green and white light operated by hand. These embryonic traffic lights were soon replaced by two-colour automatic lights at street corners controlled by time switches. The amber light was added to prevent accidents between vehicles too quick off the mark, or not quick enough to stop.

Individual time switches on traffic lights often caused as many problems as they solved, as they did not account for the overall flow of traffic through the streets of towns. So the sequencing of traffic lights was introduced which coordinated the lights to a pre-set plan.

Where traffic was sporadic, the fixed-time control of traffic lights began to give way to other schemes in the USA at the beginning of the 1930s. First, microphones were introduced at the side of the road, so drivers could activate the light change by sounding their horns. This naturally led to many objections and the system was superseded by the much more successful method of placing electrical contacts in the path of vehicles.

In Britain the familiar rubber strips across the road by traffic lights are pneumatic tubes. Compression by a vehicle running over them operates an air-activated switch by the side of the road.

Stationary vehicles at traffic lights presented a captive market to the enterprising underclasses in Manhattan, who began cleaning windscreens for a buck — often whether you wanted it or not. Some even managed to tinker with the light sequence to give themselves more time. The habit spread to other cities and now you can buy all sorts of things, from flowers to the evening newspaper, while waiting at the lights.

Motor scooter

A rather curious form of transport appeared in New York in 1915. It looked like a child's scooter with no seat and just a platform for the rider to stand on. It was called the Auto-Ped and was driven by a two-horsepower motor and had a top speed of 35 mph (55 km/h). The machine was the first of many attempts to produce small, economical run-arounds early in the century. But it remained for the Italian company Piaggio to make the first commercially successful motor scooter in 1946.

Piaggio's Vespa was nothing less than a new kind of vehicle. It was conceived during the Second World War after an air raid by the RAF had wrecked the Piaggio aircraft engine plant at Pontedera. Finding getting around the site on foot a tiring business set the boss, Enrico Piaggio, thinking. He asked one of his engineers,

Mods rode motor scooters, wore neat French clothes and long anoraks, had shortish hair and listened to the up-the-minute sounds of the Swinging Sixties. Rockers rode motorbikes, wore leathers, had long hair and listened to Chuck Berry, Eddie Cochran and Gene Vincent. They didn't like each other much and became involved in a number of fights. The most notorious of these took place on the beach at Margate on the Whitsun Bank Holiday in 1964. This press picture where one unfortunate Rocker was outnumbered by a gang of Mods was regarded at the time as a classic comment on modern British youth.

William Wilder's great 1953 location movie Roman Holiday *had Gregory Peck and Audrey Hepburn rushing about the city on one of those new scooters.*

Corradino d'Ascanio, to come up with a simple two-wheel personal transport.

Within a few weeks d'Ascanio's design was ready. It had three unique features: the frame was open, with a flat footboard; the two-stroke engine was completely enclosed; and the small wheels were carried on stub axles so that they could easily be removed without disturbing the drive.

The Vespa was well ahead of its day with its spot-welded frame and chassis-less construction — a vehicle so new that some thought it rather weird. It was practical and economical to make and the Vespa was an immediate hit. Through the 1950s and 1960s scooters became both popular and fashionable. And in the 1990s there has been a renewed success as its qualities in ever more congested cities have been discovererd by another generation.

Lipstick

The first solid lipstick appeared in the USA in 1915, manufactured by Maurice Levy. It involved a metal cartridge container with a sliding tube. The new lipstick allowed women to sport vividly coloured lips and by the 1920s women of all ages were trying lipstick for the first time.

Women and men had been colouring their lips with various dyes and chemicals for thousands of years. By the beginning of the 20th century some lip colourings were available in stick form, somewhat like a crayon. The new lipstick, however, was more to the liking of women. It was smoother to apply and could be carried around in its small convenient container.

Advertising started to promote the virtues of make-up in the 1920s and, with prices coming down all the time, cosmetics became affordable for all. More women were earning money and could afford to buy the things that made them feel good. Lipsticks became the biggest seller in the cosmetic boom that followed the First World War. The cinema also began to influence the look of women as they took their cue from the stars. When Technicolor arrived lipstick sales received another boost.

Today wearing lipstick is just a part of getting dressed and one of an array of beauty products that most women don't think twice about using.

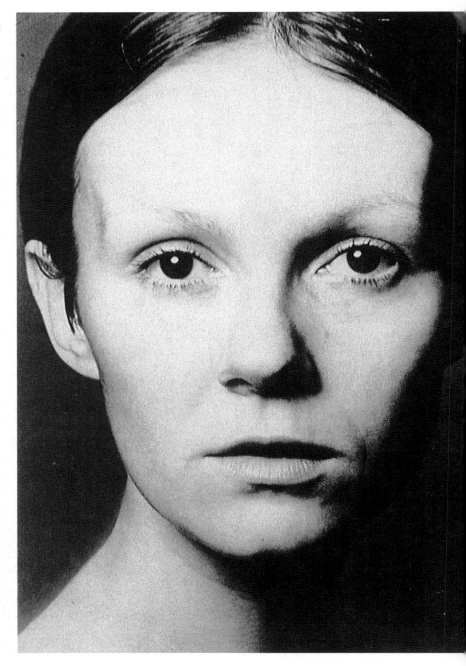

These photographs of famous French model Nicole de Lamargé before and after make-up appeared in Elle magazine on 17 March 1962. Elle began publication in 1945 and established itself as one of the most elegant of women's magazines in the French tradition. In 1959, Swiss photographer and designer Peter Knapp became the magazine's art director and began to give it a new vigour. He did away with the forced posing of the conventional fashion genre and replaced it with a radical freedom of form and spirit, with layouts of anarchic angles and twists that were to be highly influential in the new magazines of the 1960s.

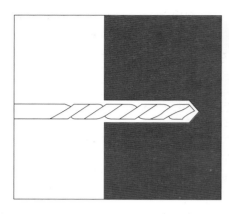

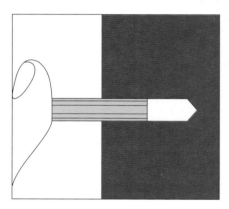

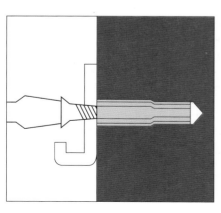

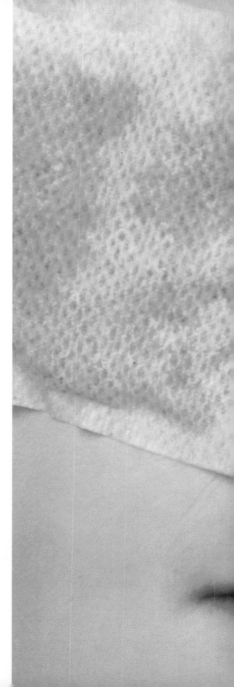

Rawlplug/molly

The Rawlplug or molly came about as a result of some refitting work being carried out at the British Museum in 1919. To meet the concerns of the museum that wall fixings should cause as little damage to the masonry as possible, the builder John J. Rawlings invented a fibre plug which could be inserted into a drilled hole to take the screw.

The traditional method of wall fixing was to chisel a hole and plug it with wood to take the screw. The new Rawlplugs, which were made out of jute bonded with pig's blood, made a much neater job. And because the plug expanded as the screw went in, it made the fit tighter and the fixing stronger.

Rawlings formed the Rawlplug Company and for a while it operated in a Kensington mews with one machine. After a heavy advertising campaign in the daily newspapers, demand became so strong that the company had to move to a larger factory in south-east London. The Rawlplug held sway until the appearance of plastic wall plugs much later in the century.

In 1934, the company made another fixing plug innovation. This was the expanding-metal Rawlbolt, the first of its kind. It had a sheath of metal that pressed outwards as the central bolt was tightened and was designed for use in concrete and masonry work.

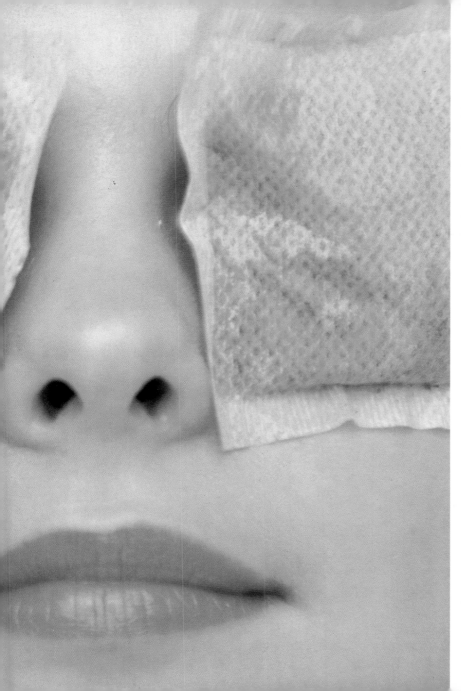

Tea bag

The first tea bags appeared in the USA in 1919, made with muslin. The idea was introduced by Joseph Kreiger in San Francisco for sampling tea. The first commercial tea bags were originally intended for caterers; by the mid-1930s most were being bought for the home. Tetley Inc. of New York was one of the early suppliers and had plans to introduce tea bags to Britain before the war. But it wasn't until 1952 that Tetley began marketing its first tea bags in the Old Country. The British, who pride themselves on their taste in tea, have always been conservative about how it should be made, and resisted the very notion of the tea bag. For many there was only one method for making a perfect cup of tea, which had been etched into the brains of generations of tea makers. This was it: warm the teapot, put in it one teaspoon of loose tea per cup and 'one for the pot', pour in freshly boiled water and leave to brew for five minutes.

Despite all this, the tea bag did gradually become accepted, and by the 1990s around 75 per cent of tea is made in Britain using tea bags. (See also Tea-maker, page 11).

Apparently having an additional benefit of some magical essence, tea bags have been used as a variation on the moisturizing effect of placing cucumber slices over the eyes in attempts to stave off the inevitable effects of ageing.

Food mixer

The first domestic food mixer with its own fixed stand and bowl was launched in 1919. It was the Model H-5 Mixer from Troy Metal Products, a subsidiary of Hobart Manufacturing in the USA, and had a unique 'planetary' mixing action, which is to say that the beater rotated in one direction while moving the bowl around in the opposite direction. The action was patented in 1920 and the machine became known as the KitchenAid.

The KitchenAid was the offspring of a baker's mixer developed in 1908 by Herbert Johnson, a designer at Hobart Manufacturing, whose machine was conceived to replace the need for mixing dough with an iron spoon. In 1910 the Hamilton Beach Manufacturing Co. also introduced an electric food mixer, but the Hobart machine made the early running and by 1917 it had become classified as standard equipment on all US Navy ships.

KitchenAids were being advertised in US national magazines during the 1920s and caught the mood of female emancipation which, among other things, demanded less toil in the kitchen. The machines were still bulky and heavy and in the 1930s Hobart recruited Egmont Arens to redesign the

The KitchenAid food mixer in the 1990s has all the same impressive characteristics of the Egmont Arens design that was introduced in the 1930s.

mixer. He made the KitchenAid more compact, softening the lines and streamlining the shape. His design was soon recognized as a classic.

In Britain it was the Kenwood Chef that came to the fore in the second half of the century. Ken Wood set up his company in a garage in Woking, Surrey in the late 1940s to make domestic appliances. The first was a toaster, followed by a kitchen mixing machine in 1948. The mixing machine particularly interested Wood and he realized that with different attachments, variable speeds and more than one power outlet it could become the essential multi-purpose kitchen gadget.

The Kenwood Chef was the result, a food processor that was a mixer, juice extractor, can opener, coffee grinder, potato peeler, liquidiser, siever and mincer all in one. Just as Hobart had given the KitchenAid the attentions of an outside designer, Kenwood enlisted British designer Kenneth Grange in the 1960s to help to enhance the appeal of the Kenwood Chef. With over eight million sold since the 1950s, it has also become a classic in its own way.

Hair dryer

Two hand-held electric hair dryers appeared in 1920, both designed and made in Racine, Wisconsin. The Cyclone, which looked little different from the hair dryers of the 1990s, came from Hamilton Beach, and the Race was made by the

Racine Universal Motor Co. Early hair dryers were made of aluminium or stainless steel with chrome. In the 1930s Bakelite became the favoured material, remaining cooler and also insulating the case. By the end of the century hair dryers were being made with a wide range of functions, for both women and men.

Chester A. Beach had made the first high-speed fractional horsepower universal electric motor in 1905 and, with Fred Osius and L. H. Hamilton, formed the Hamilton Beach Manufacturing Co. The new electric motor was developed as the basis for a number of industrial machines and domestic appliances, including the first electric-powered sewing machine in 1912, a fixed-stand electric hair dryer in 1914, a portable vacuum cleaner in 1921 and an electric blender in 1922.

Improvements to the hair dryer in the 1930s and 1940s included variable temperature settings and speeds. In 1951 the first hair dryers to be sold with plastic bonnets appeared in the USA. These allowed women to emulate at home the functions of the styling dryer in the hairdressing salon. By the 1990s all sorts of different attachments such as spiked 'voluminizers', diffusers and nozzles, so-called 'turbo fans' and a wide range of temperature settings have extended the range of at-home styling possibilities even further. Famous hair stylists such as Vidal Sassoon realized that their names should also be in the home and began to endorse hair dryers and even produce their own.

The hair dryer as sexual symbol in
Hal Ashby's 1975 *movie* Shampoo,
with Julie Christie and Warren
Beatty. Satirizing Hollywood, where
it was made, and an America just
about to elect Richard Nixon as
President, the film reflected the
bleakness of excess and wayward-
ness in a society which seemed to
have lost the 1960s ideal of free
love and reduced it just to free sex.
Julie Christie from England had
made her mark in Darling *and*
rocketed to international stardom
in Dr Zhivago. *Warren Beatty*
from America had come from
a début in Splendour in the
Grass *and a big hit,* Bonnie and
Clyde. *A certain frisson between*
them had started when they first
met in the 1971 Western McCabe
and Mrs Miller.

Motorway/ freeway

The Avus Autobahn in Berlin was planned in 1909 as a test track, race track and public road for motor traffic only, and was nearly complete when building came to a halt with the start of the First World War. It finally opened to traffic on 10 September 1921 – six miles (9.5 km) of dual carriageway and ten concrete flyovers providing the controlled access. The Avus Autobahn, which runs between Grünewald and the suburb of Wannsee, is still in use.

Autobahns were given major priority in the Third Reich. A thousand miles (1,600 km) had been completed by 1938, and 2,300 miles (3,700 km) by the Second World War. Italy started building its autostrada in the inter-war years, and the first section of the world's first inter-city motorway between Milan and Varese was opened on 21 September 1924 by the King of Italy. Mussolini backed the programme and by 1932 the network was 330 miles (530 km).

The first motorway in the USA was New York's 15-mile-long (24 km) Bronx River Parkway, opened in 1925. By 1939 the 60-mile (96 km) Queen Elizabeth Way between Toronto and Hamilton in Canada was complete and 70 miles (112 km) of motorway had also been opened in the Netherlands. In Britain the first eight-mile (13 km) section of the M6 did not open until 5 December 1958.

ARCETTI

TORNEY

abc

After a bizarre low-speed pursuit along Los Angeles freeways, which was televised live nationally, O. J. Simpson was arrested on 17 June 1994 for the murder of his ex-wife Nicole Brown and her friend Ronald Goldman four days earlier. That day Simpson had taken a mysterious flight to Chicago, was questioned by police on his return but soon released. The American football player turned movie star was unquestionably a hero to many Black Americans and the trial that ensued exposed all the frailties and absurdities of American paranoia, prejudice and political correctness. Conducted in front of a national television audience, the 'Trial of the Century' often came across as soap-opera entertainment rather than justice in action. After 16 months, the jury returned a not-guilty verdict and O. J. Simpson was set free. In a final twist, Simpson was found liable to the death of his wife in a civil action brought by his in-laws. So one verdict said he didn't do it and one verdict said he did.

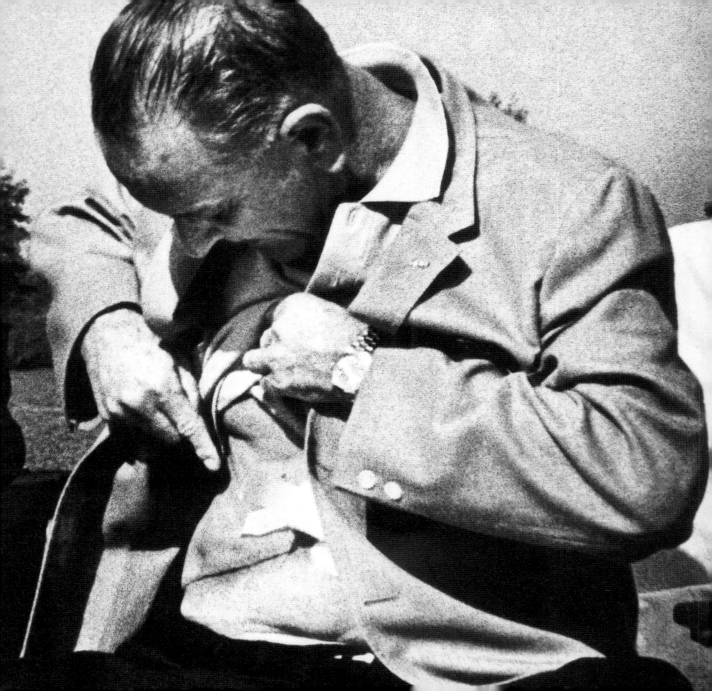

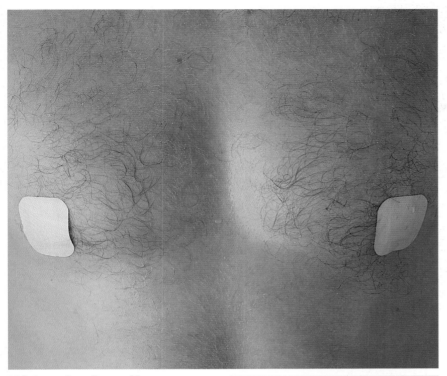

Male joggers have discovered how to prevent their nipples from getting sore.

Left: *Lyndon Johnson shows off his plasters after the removal of his gallstones and kidney stones. Texan 'LBJ' was sworn in as President after the assassination of John F. Kennedy in 1963 and won the Presidential election in the following year with a huge majority. He continued Kennedy's reforms aimed at improving the position of Blacks in American society, but the escalation of the war in Vietnam led to pressure on his policies and growing unpopularity. In 1968 he announced that he would not be seeking a second term. He died in 1973 at the age of 71.*

Band-Aid/ Elastoplast

Johnson & Johnson had been making adhesive surgical tape and gauze separately for years when in 1920 Earle E. Dickson, a cotton buyer in the purchase department, thought to put the two together in a ready-made strip that could be cut as required and applied quickly and easily. The name Band-Aid is credited to W. Johnson Kenyon, the superintendent of the company's textile mill.

According to company lore, Dickson had become tired of having continually to dress his accident-prone wife's fingers, which she often burned or cut in the kitchen. Determined to find a less laborious way of dressing the wounds, he laid a strip of the company's surgical tape on a table, sticky side up. He then placed small pads of the company's gauze at intervals along the tape. This assembly was covered with a backing of crinoline, and then rolled up. Whenever his wife needed a bandage he could simply cut a piece off the roll.

The first 'J&J Band-Aid Adhesive Bandages' were produced in 1921. Sales were slow until 1924, when mechanization of the production process allowed Band-Aids to be sold in three-inch pre-cut strips. Further improvements were the addition of holes over the gauze section of the tape to allow the wound to breathe, the medication of the gauze and the individual packing of single plasters. The entire product was made sterile in 1939.

Smith & Nephew's Elastoplast, which was first made in 1924, has achieved much the same generic status in other parts of the world as Band-Aid has in America. The rights to the name were shared with Beiersdorf AG of Germany between 1931 and 1951, with Smith & Nephew holders in Britain and the British Empire. By 1932 there were 14 varieties of Elastoplast. In 1946 Waterproof Elastoplast was launched and Airstrip soon followed. It remains market leader in Britain and prominent in Australasia, South Africa and Canada.

Jubilee clip

This clever little hose clip tightened by a worm-drive was invented in 1921 by Commander Lumley-Robinson, founder of L. Robinson and Co. of Gillingham, Kent. By 1993 it was being exported to 42 countries for use in the motor industry, aerospace, nuclear power, agriculture, the armed forces – in fact wherever engineering hoses are found. By the end of the 1990s well over two billion Jubilee clips had been made.

Behind the success of the Jubilee clip lies the indomitable figure of Mrs Emily Lumley-Robinson, wife of the inventor. It was she who sold their house to raise the capital required for the original tooling and materials of the venture. After her husband died in 1939 she took over the reins of the firm and, in the face of all the prevailing prejudices of the time, ran it with great energy and success.

With an all-female workforce, she met the massive demands of the War Department during the Second World War when Jubilee clips were being used at the rate of a million a month in military aircraft alone. Such was her commitment to the cause that, after hearing an Air Ministry appeal on the radio in 1941, she sent a cheque for £5,000 for the purchase of a Spitfire for the RAF.

In 1948 the Lumley-Robinsons' son John became managing director of the firm, but Emily continued to work on until 1982, when at the age of 97 she was forced to retire because of ill health.

Ice lolly/ Popsicle

The iced lollipop was the invention of Frank Epperson of Oakland, California, who patented the idea in 1923. He sold the patent to the food-processing company Joe Lowe, which launched the lollipops under the band name Popsicle, a name that soon became generic for all ice lollies in America.

The invention of the ice lolly was not the result of any concerted research. Epperson was a lemonade-mix salesman. He had been demonstrating his product one afternoon to prospective customers in New Jersey and he inadvertently left a glass of the lemonade with a spoon in it on a window sill. The night that followed was cold and the temperature plunged to below zero. In the morning Epperson discovered his glass of lemonade still sitting where he had left it. He pulled the spoon out of the glass, and found that he had a prototype ice lolly in his hands.

Harri Peccinotti's photographs for the 1969 Pirelli calendar. Launched in 1963 as an up-market take-off on the pin-up calendars traditionally handed out to garages and tyre dealers, the Pirelli calendars quickly gained a reputation for the quality of their imagery, art direction and design which has made them collectors' items. Photographers who have worked on the calendar include Terence Donovan, Peter Knapp, Barry Lategan and Sarah Moon.

In his later life Howard Hughes became so obsessive about germs that he ordered Kleenex tissues to be put down on the floor of his home so that they could be thrown away after people had walked on them. In 1923 Hughes inherited from his father the rights to a type of drill bit used in practically every oilfield in the world, which made him unbelievably rich. He first hit the headlines as a Hollywood playboy, then film-maker. He became a dare-devil pilot, aircraft maker and finally an eccentric recluse. He died in an air crash in 1976 at the age 70.

Cotton swabs

Cottons swabs on a stick called Baby Gays were introduced in 1925. In 1926 the name became Q-tips Baby Gays and eventually just Q-tips. Originally designed to clean baby ears, noses and mouths and to oil tender skin, they also became popular for other uses such as first aid and beauty care.

After serving in the US Army during the First World War, Polish-born Leo Gerstenzang became associated with the Red Cross and met ex-President Herbert Hoover, who asked him to assist in the Relief Administration's rehabilitation efforts in Europe.

In 1922 he returned to the USA and founded the Leo Gerstenzang Infant Novelty Co., selling accessories for baby care. A year later he was watching his wife looking after their baby daughter when he saw her put a piece of cotton on to a toothpick to

Paper tissues

In 1924 Kimberly-Clark introduced soft paper tissues called Celluwipes, for removing make-up. Sales did nothing to excite. When it was realized that they were mainly being used to wipe and blow noses the company relaunched the product, calling it first Kleenex-Kerchiefs and then simply Kleenex.

Kimberly-Clark started business with a small pulp mill in the forest of Wisconsin to produce newsprint. After expansion in the paper business, the company began to look to diversify. At the beginning of the First World War an entirely new paper product

emerged, called cellulose wadding. It was originally developed for medical dressings as a substitute for cotton wool. The US Army started using what came to be called Cellucotton; it was soft and more absorbent than cotton wool, and remained strong when wet.

It was the boom in cosmetics after the war (see Lipstick, page 46) that set the Kimberly-Clark people thinking about a new use for their Cellucotton. When Kleenex for noses was introduced Cellucotton found its true calling. For the rest of the century, with new packaging, new sizes and the introduction of recycled material, Kleenex has remained the soft paper tissue market leader – and the generic name for paper handkerchiefs.

use as an applicator. He immediately put his mind to the challenge of making a ready-to-use cotton swab entirely by automatic machine.

For several years Gerstenzang experimented until he had perfected his machine. Using carefully selected and cured non-splintering birchwood, it wrapped cotton uniformly around both of the blunted ends. It then packed the swabs in sliding-tray boxes, which allowed them to be taken out one at a time. It also sterilized and sealed the boxes with a glassine wrapper. 'Untouched by human hands' thus became a most persuasive slogan for promoting Q-tips.

In 1946 Q-tips SA was formed in Paris and the company also expanded into Canada shortly after. In 1958 the British makers of lollipop sticks, Papersticks Ltd, was acquired and its machinery was taken back to America where it was adapted for the manufacture of paper stick swabs. This allowed the development of Q-tips with biodegradable paper-and-wood sticks.

Q-tips was the only product of its kind until 1941. Its main competitor, Johnson & Johnson's Cotton Buds, market leader in Britain and elsewhere, have always had plastic sticks. In America Q-tips retained 60 per cent of the market into the 1990s.

Q-tips were originally meant for cleaning babies, but people latched on to hundreds of other uses, from model making and cleaning machine parts, guns and fishing reels to restoring furniture and paintings – or Tiffany lamps.

Pop-up toaster

Burnt toast was the problem of early electric toasters. You had to stand over them watching and checking all the time. The first toaster with an in-built thermostat that automatically ejected the toast when it was nicely brown was invented by Charles Strite, a mechanic from Stillwater, Minnesota. It was introduced by McGraw Electric of Minneapolis in June 1926.

GEC in the USA had brought out an electric toaster in 1913, with bare wires around strips of insulating mica which glowed red hot. But it could only toast one side of the bread at a time. Others followed, some automatically turning the toast. But they were all hand operated, and all prone to delivering a black, charred crisp and a white pall of smoke.

When sliced bread become the norm in America the standard size of a slice helped the toaster to become an indispensable item in the kitchen. The Toastmaster was introduced to Britain in 1928, although pop-up toasters did not become widespread in Europe until the 1950s.

Toaster, 1967, a screenprint by the influential British artist Richard Hamilton. His work expressed various aspects of popular culture and for many he was the first true Pop artist. He helped to organize the 1956 Whitechapel Gallery exhibition 'This is Tomorrow'. Later he taught in Newcastle and also organized the Duchamp exhibition at the Tate in 1966.

hamilton

Aerosol

The aerosol was invented in 1926 by Norwegian engineer Erik Rothheim. Soon after, paint and polish manufacturer Alf Bjerke began to make the first commercial aerosols in Oslo while insecticide aerosols were also made for a time by Norwegian instrument makers, Frode Mortensen. But neither enterprise was a success and the aerosol seemed destined for the failed-invention file until the Americans took up the cause in the Second World War.

While fighting in the Pacific theatre, the US Army came up against disease-carrying insects that were doing them more harm than the Japanese. Research chemist L. D. Goodhue had been experimenting with aerosols on and off since 1935, and in 1941 he had conducted a successful experiment which involved pitting an insecticide dispensed by aerosol against a cageful of cockroaches. The cockroaches lost.

In 1942 the US Army began to be supplied with 'bug bombs'. These were aerosol canisters containing insecticide and around 50 million were made during the war. Word about aerosols – and some actual army canisters – got out after the war and demand from civilians began to grow for the handy cans. The first commercial aerosols using lightweight casing materials and plastic valves were made by Airosol Inc in Kansas on 21st November 1946. By the 1990s world annual production of aerosols had reached billions.

Aerosol cans contain particles of anything from furniture polish to deodorant, which are packed under pressure with an inert gas. Pushing down on the release button sends a fine spray of whatever it is shooting out of the nozzle propelled by the pressurized gas. A family of gases called CFCs (chlorofluorocarbons) was the preferred propellant for aerosols – until something rather serious started to happen.

In the stratosphere is a layer of the gas ozone which stops harmful radiation from the sun reaching the Earth. CFCs released into the atmosphere slowly rise into the stratosphere where the radiation breaks them down into chlorine. This chlorine reacts with and destroys the ozone, causing holes to appear in the ozone layer. The increased radiation that is let in has been responsible for the rise in the occurrence of skin cancer towards the end of the century (see also Suntan lotion, page 91). In June 1990, 93 nations agreed to phase out production of CFCs and other ozone-depleting chemicals by the end of the century.

Overleaf: The aerosol became the paintbrush of the graffiti artist, and every city in the world has become the canvas. Nowhere has this art excelled more than in New York and this was celebrated in the 1974 book **Watching my name go by,** *with photographs of graffiti on subway trains and buses by Jon Narr, commentary by Norman Mailer and design by Mervyn Kurlansky.*

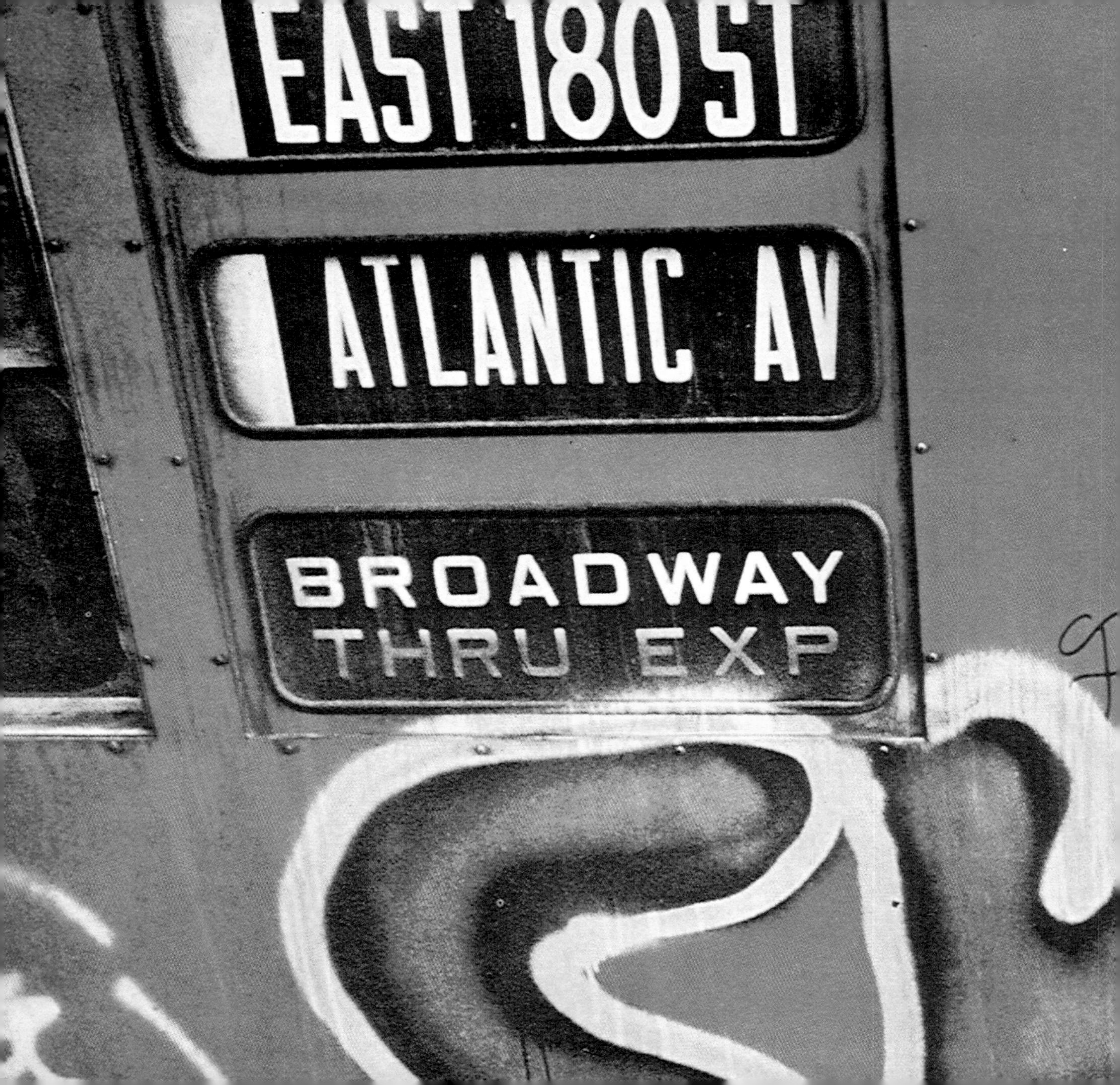
EAST 180 ST
ATLANTIC AV
BROADWAY
THRU EXP

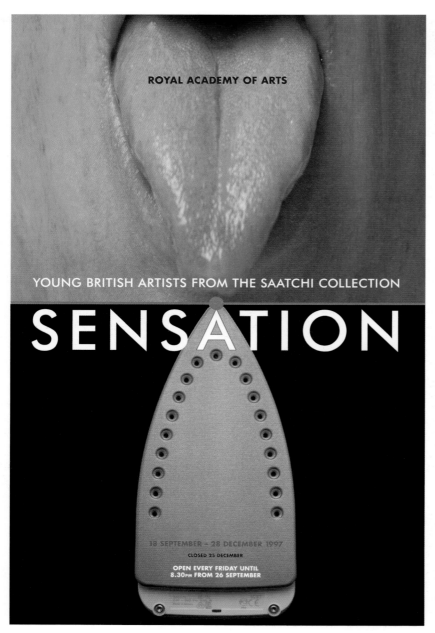

ROYAL ACADEMY OF ARTS

YOUNG BRITISH ARTISTS FROM THE SAATCHI COLLECTION

SENSATION

18 SEPTEMBER - 28 DECEMBER 1997

CLOSED 25 DECEMBER

OPEN EVERY FRIDAY UNTIL
8.30PM FROM 26 SEPTEMBER

Steam iron

A domestic steam iron was introduced by a New York dry-cleaning company called Eldec in 1926, but it was not until much later in the century that the technology was ready for steam irons to be safe and reliable enough for general acceptance. Thermostatic temperature controls were introduced in 1936 and better methods were gradually developed for delivering the steam evenly to the fabric.

In 1952 Hoover introduced a steam iron with automatic temperature control that became the standard for years. It had a sole plate which was made of die-cast aluminium with a satin finish and grooves that distributed the steam evenly over the fabric. The design of the handle had both right- and left-hand thumb rests. There was also an automatic shut-off so that no steam could be produced when the iron was placed on its heel. Further innovations since then, such as non-stick sole plates and spot steam nozzles, have gradually overcome people's resistance to steam irons and now over 80 per cent of electric irons sold are steam.

The 'Sensation' exhibition at the Royal Academy in London in 1997 left some people rather hot under the collar, mainly because of the graphic piece depicting the 'Moors Murderer' Myra Hindley by Marcus Harvey. The show was of young British artists taken from Maurice Saatchi's private collection. The poster was designed by Why Not Associates.

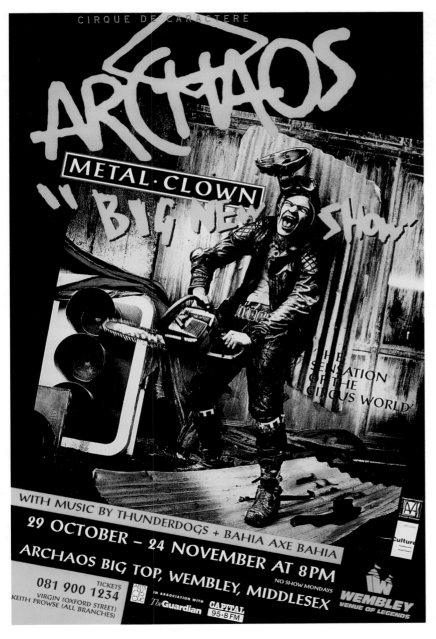

Chainsaw

In 1927, on the wooded slopes of Mount Dolmar in Thuringia, Germany, Emil Lerp demonstrated the first petrol-engine sawing machine for forestry work. The chainsaw company that Lerp founded took its name from that moment and Dolmar GmbH of Hamburg is today one of the leading manufacturers of chainsaws in the world, selling in over 100 countries.

Before Emil Lerp had demonstrated his mobile chainsaw, Andreas Stihl had founded a company in Stuttgart also with the objective of developing a chainsaw. In 1926 he produced an electrically driven machine suitable for sawmills and forestry yards. In 1929 Stihl's company introduced its first chainsaw with a petrol engine called the 'Stihl tree felling machine'.

Chainsaws have transformed what used to be very laborious work in forests and woods, allowing cutting and clearing at rates unheard of at the beginning of the century. Yet the early machines needed more than one man to handle them. Stihl's dream had always been to develop a machine light enough to be operated by one person. His company achieved this in 1950 with the Stihl BL, which led to the best-selling Stihl Contra in 1959.

The French adult fun fair Archaos, which travels around Europe, features erotic and violent anarchy, including the Metal Clown who juggles with running chainsaws.

Electric razor

Schick Dry Shaver Inc. patented and marketed the first electric dry-shaver system in 1929. It had the market all to itself until 1934, when Remington introduced its first model. By the middle of the 1930s over a million shavers had been sold in the USA. In 1994 the annual market for electric shavers worldwide had reached 32 million.

In the early part of the century Jacob Schick was a soldier who had become ill while stationed in the Philippines. On doctor's orders to move to a colder climate he went to Alaska. It was gold fever time and, like many others, Schick went to seek his fortune. While looking for gold he found shaving with soap in icy water was not the most comfortable experience and he turned his mind to making a dry shaver. His first effort was based on a barber's hair trimmer, but no manufacturer was interested.

When the First World War broke out, Schick rejoined the army and rose to the rank of lieutenant-colonel. In 1919, back in civilian life, he again set about his old task of developing a dry shaver. By 1928 his prototypes were far enough advanced for him to raise money for production development. This he did by selling his Magazine Repeating Razor Co., which was based on another of his inventions, the safety razor blade dispenser. A year later 'Colonel' Schick, as he had become known in the business, finally

Sliced bread

Without sliced bread, where would the club sandwich be; without the club sandwich where would the American diner be?

It took 26 years for Otto Frederick Rohwedder's idea for a bread-slicing machine to become accepted. He started work on his first in 1912. In 1915 he was told by his doctor that he had only a year to live. In 1917 he lost his prototype and all his tools and equipment in a fire. In 1922, still alive, he secured new financial backing. In January 1928 he produced a machine that sliced bread and wrapped it to keep the moisture in. And in May 1928 it was this machine that was used by a local bakery in Battle Creek, Michigan to produce the first pre-sliced, wrapped loaf of bread.

In 1928 the Continental Bakery of New York had also introduced Wonder Bread, the first wrapped loaf to be distributed throughout the USA. In 1930 the company bought some of Rohwedder's machines and Wonder Bread began to appear pre-sliced. That same year sliced and wrapped bread also began to be sold in the north of England.

By 1933 around 80 per cent of all bread sold in the USA was sliced and wrapped. Americans loved it and, without irony, the phrase 'the best thing since sliced bread' was coined.

fulfilled his life-long dream.

In Europe just before the Second World War Braun in Germany and Philips in the Netherlands both introduced dry shavers. In the post-war recovery, Philishave renewed development of its rotary shavers, invented by Alexandre Horowitz, and in 1951 Braun enlisted the designers Dieter Rams and Gerd Alfred Müller to refresh its foil-head models. The stage was set for five contenders to battle it out for world supremacy: Remington, Schick and Sunbeam from the USA, and Braun and Philips from Europe. By the 1990s Philips had 50 per cent of the European market and 55 per cent of the American market. Second in Europe is Braun and in America it is Remington.

Early on, women began to borrow men's electric razors for their legs, armpits and other parts. So naturally shavers designed expressly for them was the next step. Remington's Duchess was the first, in 1940, and Philips Ladyshave followed ten years later. Since the 1980s most electric shavers have been cordless.

Victor Kiam bought Remington in 1979. The company had lost $30 million over the five preceding years and his canny marketing turned it round, doubling market share and increasing sales tenfold. He became a household name writing and presenting Remington's television commercials with the famous line 'I liked it so much I bought the company', which earned him all sorts of plaudits including an American Academy of Achievement Award.

Victor Kiam: 'Hello'

'I liked this'

'The Remington Microscreen rechargeable'

'I liked the shaver so much I bought the company'

'It shaves incredibly close'

'Shaves as close as a blade or your money back.'

Frozen food

The technique of freezing fish was developed in Halifax, Nova Scotia by Dr Archibald Huntsman who began work on the project at the Fisheries Experimental Station in 1926. In January 1929 one-pound (half kilo) packs of frozen haddock were made available for sale in Toronto by the Biological Board of Canada under the name of Fresh Ice Fillets. The innovation was a hit and soon the fillets were being shipped to Toronto at a rate of 1,000 pounds (500 kg) a week. The Canadian frozen fish enterprise grew quickly. Other varieties were added and shipments extended as far west as the Prairies. But the technique of freezing remained confined to fish. It was Clarence Birdseye who was to broaden the range and popularity of frozen food. Between 1912 and 1915 he had been engaged in a US government survey of fish and wildlife in Labrador, Newfoundland. There he reported seeing natives catching fish which froze solid as soon as they were landed and he also learned to preserve vegetables by putting them in a tub of water and freezing them.

In 1924 Clarence Birdseye established the General Seafoods Corporation in Gloucester, Massachusetts to develop

Inuit fishing in Hudson Bay, Canada, in the 1990s. The fish freeze almost at once, a point that was also noted by frozen-food originator Clarence Birdseye on a trip to Labrador early in the century.

these processes commercially. Five years later he sold out to the Postum Company for $22 million. Part of the deal was that the Birdseye name should be split into two to make the new brand name. In 1930 Birds Eye launched its first range consisting of various frozen fish and meats, peas, spinach, raspberries, loganberries and cherries.

By 1933 there were 516 frozen-food stores in the USA. In 1939 various frozen pre-cooked dishes with chicken, beef and turkey were introduced by Birds Eye and other manufacturers.

Scotch tape/ Sellotape

The problem of making a waterproof tape for sealing packaging became the concern of 3M laboratory worker Richard G. Drew. He heard about Cellophane, which had just been introduced, and in June 1929 he ordered 100 yards of the new moisture-proof material. It was cut it into 6-inch (15 cm) widths for the adhesive to be applied, which proved to be very difficult. 3M persevered and on 8 September 1930 the first roll of Scotch tape was made. To begin with Scotch tape was marketed to grocers, meat packers and bakers, but did not do too well. Then it was launched by 3M to consumers somewhat tentatively during the Depression when Americans were unlikely to risk

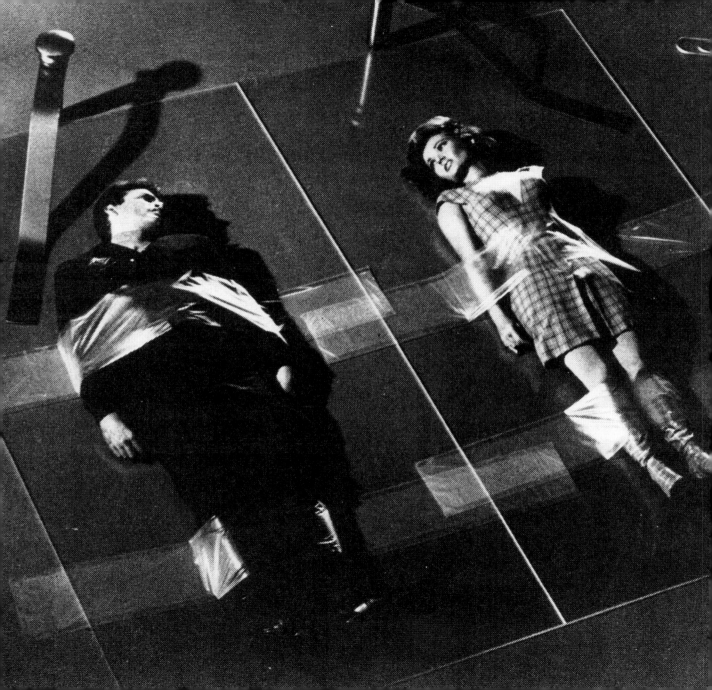

Our hero and heroine are stuck with familiar-looking transparent tape in the 1960s TV series Land of the Giants.

their money on untried products. But the prevailing thriftiness of that era was in fact the making of the tape which was so useful in mending and fixing things. People found more uses for the tape than 3M had ever imagined.

Scotch tape's great rival in world markets is Sellotape, which was created in England by Colin Kininmonth and George Gray in 1937. They also coated Cellophane and used rubber resin as the adhesive, basing their technique on a French patent. Today Sellotape is brand leader in Britain and Europe's biggest selling clear cellulose tape. Meanwhile Scotch tape entered the 1990s with 90 per cent of the US market and has been the mainstay of 3M.

Scrabble

Scrabble was devised in 1931 by Alfred Mosher Butts, an architect from Rhinebeck, New York, who was unemployed like so many millions during the Great Depression. Butts determined the value of the letters by counting the number of times they were used on a single page of the *New York Times*. He was never really any good at the game himself, which he originally called Criss-Cross, and his wife Nina used to beat him regularly, once scoring 234 points with the word 'quixotic'.

After being turned down by a number of manufacturers, Butts decided to market the game himself. He went into partnership with James Brunot, a retired government official, who produced the sets in his garage in Danbury, Connecticut. They changed the name of the game to Lexico and began to sell it in 1946, making 200 sets a week by hand. Two years later Selchow & Righter acquired the rights and started to mass produce the game,

Scrabble exercises the minds of retired people, who have time on their hands and also have accumulated the vocabulary to explore the boundaries of the game's possibilities.

changing its name to Scrabble.

Butts received a royalty of five cents for each game sold, and by the time the copyright expired in 1974 this was giving him an income of $50,000 a year. When Butts died in 1993, 100 million sets of Scrabble had been sold worldwide.

Anglepoise/ Luxo lamp

George Carwardine, an English engineer who specialized in car suspension systems and shock absorbers, designed a task lamp in 1932 for clipping to engineering benches. He based the mechanics of the lamp on the jointing principles of the human arm, using springs to counterbalance the members so that the lamp could direct light to any position in three planes. He approached the Midlands family firm of Herbert Terry and Sons, experts in spring manufacturing, and production began in 1933.
No attempt was ever made to style the lamp, but the Anglepoise became a classic of rational design, and it has sold in Britain for over 60 years in tens of thousands.

The design should have guaranteed the manufacturer and designer worldwide success. Unfortunately the Terry family failed to foresee the value of what to them was a sideline to their main business and they granted a manufacturing licence after the Second World War to their Scandinavian agent, a Norwegian called Jac Jacobsen.

The original 1933 Anglepoise lamp designed by George Carwardine and made by Herbert Terry and Sons. Carwardine wanted to call his new lamp the 'Equipoise', but the name could not be registered as a trademark as it already existed in the English language.

Jacobsen launched the lamp in the USA as the Luxo in 1951 and, after the US patent ran out in 1953, Luxo's operation reached a turnover of $1 million in eight years. In 1971 Herbert Terry and Sons was acquired by the Associated Spring Corporation of the USA, but the Terry family bought back the Anglepoise part of the business in 1975. The Anglepoise lamp thus remains British, although the design has been imitated under different names all over the world.

Soap opera

Washing-powder manufacturers in the USA began to sponsor radio dramas in the 1930s that characteristically involved never-ending stories of extraordinary events befalling quite ordinary folk with extraordinary frequency. These were broadcast live by actors who were not always of the highest calibre. This, nevertheless, gave them a certain quality, and the 'soap operas' proved to be addictive. The first soap operas (although the term was not coined until 1939) were NBC's *Betty and Bob* and *One Man's Family*, which both began in 1932.

The first American television soap was *A Woman to Remember*, produced in New York in 1947. *One Man's Family* converted from radio to television in 1949, but only survived to 1952 (the radio version endured to 1959). The first television show to become a nationwide hit was CBS's *Search for Tomorrow*, which

started in 1951 and ran for 31 years. Hollywood produced a succession of classic television soap operas, starting with *Peyton Place* in the 1960s, then *Dallas* in the 1970s and *Dynasty* in the 1980s, all of which won huge audiences worldwide.

The Hollywood soaps changed the rules by using increasingly rich and privileged families for their subjects. *Peyton Place* was set in a well-to-do New England town where apparently respectable people turned out to be full of guilty secrets and all the children seemed to have different fathers from the ones they were meant to. The oil-rich families of *Dallas* had women looking as though they had been air-

On the set of Peyton Place, the first television soap opera to command a worldwide audience: Ed Nelson, Christopher Connelly, Barbara Parkins, Tim O'Connor, Ryan O'Neil and Mia Farrow. The show, based on Grace Metalious' novel, ran for 514 episodes.

brushed and spoilt-child men trying to outdo each other for malice. The trend reached a climax with the million-dollar-an-episode *Dynasty*. Australia became adept at the more homely side of the genre and *Neighbours* became the world's most successful newcomer in the 1980s.

But the longest running TV soap in the world is *Coronation Street*, produced by Granada in Britain. It came

from an idea by Tony Warren, who still gets a credit with each show. The first half-hour episode went out at 7 p.m. on Friday, 9 December 1960, and began to be networked nationally the following spring. It has been shown twice a week ever since. By 1967 it was attracting audiences of 20 million and being sold all over the world. By the middle of 1998 *Coronation Street* had clocked up over 4,400 shows, with no sign of it ever coming to an end.

The original radio soap format is still with us, and the longest running is BBC Radio 4's *The Archers*, which has been broadcast regularly since 1 January 1951. Godfrey Baseley, a farming producer, conceived the idea of a rural drama series as an alternative to the rather solemn agricultural programmes aimed at increasing food production after the war. Today four million listeners a week tune in at lunchtime for the 'everyday story of country folk'. It has remained topical and well researched on farming matters, although its 'official' agricultural role was dropped in the early 1970s. By 1997 12,000 episodes had been broadcast, into which the producers had managed to squeeze six generations of the Archer family.

When one of the first ever radio soaps, **One Man's Family,** *transferred to television in 1949, it was not with the members of the radio cast who had established the show in the affections of listeners. They were left to carry on as before on radio, while a new televisual family was recruited.*

Mars Bar

Forrest E. Mars, the son of an American confectioner, came to England in 1932. With him he brought a recipe for a new kind of confection – the Mars Bar. It had a layer of nougat, a layer of caramel and was covered by thick milk chocolate. It was revolutionary; until then all chocolate confectionery had simply been blocks of solid chocolate.

Mars started to produce Mars Bars in a small rented factory in Slough. He sold the first hand-made Mars Bars locally at 2d. each. By the end of the first year Mars Confections Ltd. was employing 100 people. In 1961 a second factory was opened in Slough and today the company employs some 2,300 and makes three million Mars Bars a day.

The taste for Mars Bars spread during the Second World War when they were distributed to armed forces throughout the world. When post-war rationing ended, heavy advertising with the slogan 'A Mars a day helps you work, rest and play' put the Mars Bar into an unassailable position as the number-one confectionery bar.

The *Financial Times* has called the Mars Bar a more reliable currency than gold because it contains the world's basic commodities: cocoa, milk, sugar and vegetable fats.

High-profile sports sponsorship covers every angle. Mars was the official sponsor for the London Marathon in 1988.

Coat shirt

In 1932 Cecil Gee introduced the first formal shirt that buttoned all the way down the front so that it could be put it on like a coat. It also had a collar attached and was originally meant for the working-class lads of the East End of London, who didn't know how or want to attach a separate collar. The new shirts came with a diagram showing how to tie a tie.

Until the 1930s, most men's shirts were based on the design of the dress shirt, with a buttoned opening just big enough for the shirt to be pulled on over the head. This not only messed up your hair but also made the shirt prone to tearing. And if all the buttons were not carefully undone before pulling it on, they tended to fall off. Once the shirt was on a separate collar involving fiddly studs, one at the back and one at the front, had to be attached.

Cecil Gee's first shop opened in 1929 in London's Commercial Road, from where he sold his first coat shirts and also introduced the first two-piece ready-to-wear suits. After the war he introduced the American look, with imported satin shirts, wide ties, hats and shoes. He also brought the Italian look to London with its high-buttoning jackets, smart suits and narrow ties.

Such is the circular nature of trends in fashion that in the 1980s old-style shirts with no collars and dress-shirt fronts, accurately known as Grandad shirts, became popular with the young.

The shirt and Ursula Andress as Honeychile in Dr No, the first ever James Bond film. Made in 1962, it introduced 007, played by Sean Connery, and set the formula for a series that continued for the rest of the century.

Polythene

Of the many plastics that have characterized the new products of the 20th century, polyethylene is one of the most prevalent. In 1933 ICI chemist R. O. Gibson produced the polymer of ethylene gas, a white solid called polyethylene. It was easily moulded, tough, inert and water-resistant, and the company gave it its commercial name polythene. It was first used to insulate a cable connecting the Isle of Wight with the mainland across the Solent. By 1939 ICI had established a commercial plant which was producing 200 tons of polythene a week.

In the USA polyethylene slag, an oil refinery by-product, became the basis of the Tupperware phenomenon. Earl Silas Tupper, a chemist at Du Pont, was interested in producing plastic from waste materials and he finally came up with the plastic that allowed him to found the Tupperware Plastics Co. in 1938.

In Britain polythene jumped into public consciousness in 1948 when washing-up bowls made of the plastic were introduced. A type of polyethylene which is more rigid at low temperatures and softer at higher temperatures was first made by the German chemist Karl Ziegler. Today polyethylene is familiar around the world in packaging, bottles, pipes and tubing as well as toys and electrical insulation.

It's reckoned that a Tupperware party starts somewhere in the world every three seconds or so – this one was on Merseyside. In 1951 Earl Silas Tupper hired direct sellers to concentrate on taking his Tupperware around to people's homes. One of these was Brownie Wise, who started organizing the first Tupperware parties, informal get-togethers of neighbours at which Tupperware was demonstrated and sold while new recruits were made to the sales force. They came to Britain in 1960.

Tampons

When Tampax was introduced in 1934, the question that exercised many mothers was whether their daughters would remain virgins if they used the new devices. It was not something that concerned anybody by the end of the century. The Tampax prototype was made and patented by Dr Earle Haas in 1931. It consisted of compressed surgical cotton with a cord stitched through its length for sanitary removal, and a cardboard applicator to make insertion easier. Substitute plastic for cardboard and the design has hardly changed since.

For centuries women had been left to deal with menstruation as best they could. Home-made tampons had been contrived since at least Egyptian times, when women are known to have used softened papyrus leaves. Otherwise pieces of cloth or towels were worn, often precariously, for protection.

In 1921 Smith & Nephew intro-

Dyed Mohican hairstyles, leather clothes, chains, rings, hooks — and tampons as earrings: these were the Punks, a peculiarly British phenomenon of the late 1970s and early 1980s. Punks represented a complete alternative sub-culture, and the resonance is still detectable at the end of the century in contemporary art and music. However, the 1980s stereotypes ended up as little more than tourist attractions on the streets of London while adorning picture postcards alongside other clichés such as Big Ben, Beefeaters and red buses.

duced a disposable sanitary towel called Dr White's. Although hardly convenient, requiring a belt to keep it in place, it nevertheless had the advantage of staying put and being disposable; neither of which qualities had been available before.

Earle Haas was a country doctor in Colorado. His wife was a nurse and someone who absolutely hated sanitary pads. It was this that spurred him to devise a disposable sanitary tampon. Within a month of his patent being granted he was contacted by a Denver doctor, Gertrude Tenderich. She and a syndicate of backers bought the rights for $32,000. They formed the Tampax Corporation and Tenderich made the first tampons herself at home using a sewing machine and a hand-operated compressor.

Selling the new product proved anything but easy. Pharmacists, who were mainly men, were embarrassed to carry such an intimate female item, and a number of churchmen denounced tampons for destroying the evidence of virginity and encouraging masturbation. But with the medical profession in favour, Tampax began the process of education by employing women to sell door-to-door.

Sales did not really pick up until 1937 when Tampax embarked on a heavy magazine advertising campaign reaching 45 million people in America. The company began to expand rapidly with new production plants overseas and by 1940 Tampax was available in 100 countries.

Fluorescent lighting

The 'fluorescent lumiline lamp – a laboratory experiment of great promise' was introduced by the USA's General Electric Company at the annual convention of the Illuminating Engineering Society in Cincinnati, Ohio in September 1935. The hot cathode, gas-filled device was a two-foot (0.6 m) tube that emitted a bright green light.

On 23 November 1936, the US Patent Office held its centenary dinner in Washington DC and the banqueting hall was appropriately lit by GEC's fluorescent lamps, the first practical application of this novel form of lighting. Fluorescent lamps by both GEC and its rival Westinghouse were launched commercially on 1 April 1938. GEC's lamps were initially available in three wattages, three lengths and seven different colours.

The fight scene between Darth Vader and Luke Skywalker from The Empire Strikes Back, *second in the Star Wars trilogy, using light swords that looked for all the world like fluorescent tubes. Star Wars came out in 1977. As an epic struggle between good and evil the idea is as old as the hills. What was new was the special-effects setting that took the space-adventure genre out of the studio and seemingly on to location for the first time. The series was re-released with a state-of-the-art effects make-over in the 1990s.*

Monopoly

Mrs Elizabeth Phillips of Virginia devised a board game in 1924 called the Landlord's Game and although not a great success there was something about it that fascinated Charles Darrow, a heating engineer from Germantown, Pennsylvania, who was unemployed during the Depression. He decided to develop the game and call it Monopoly. The first sets were ready at the end of 1935, and eventually it became the biggest selling board game ever, and Charles Darrow became a millionaire. By the late 1990s over 150 million sets had been sold worldwide.

Darrow developed his original Monopoly game using household items and bits of wood. The counters were charms from his wife's bracelet and he chose the streets names from Atlantic City, one of the Darrow family's favourite holiday spots. Despite an initial rejection from the game manufacturers Parker Brothers, he was so convinced of the worth of his idea that he set up his own business, and in 1934 commissioned 5,000 sets to be made in Philadelphia.

The game proved very popular locally and Parker Brothers soon changed their minds. They did a deal with Darrow and had the first sets

The British Monopoly Championships have been traditionally held in one of the train stations that appear as properties in the London-based version of the game.

coming off the production lines in October 1935, ready for Christmas. Soon the head of Parker Brothers was calling it 'the hottest fad game ever known'.

The first foreign version followed when Waddington's introduced a British Monopoly in 1936, using London streets and railways, and money in pounds sterling. Since then the game has been translated into 19 languages. The Japanese version is set in Tokyo, the Greek version in Athens, and this most capitalist of games even became popular in Soviet Russia with a Moscow version.

Whatever the translation, the Boardwalk square has always remained the most expensive property – Mayfair in the London version, rue de la Paix in Paris and Paseo del Prado in Madrid. In 1972, Atlantic City put forward plans to change the names of Baltic Avenue and Mediterranean Avenue, two streets that also feature on the Monopoly board. There was such an outcry from fans of the game that they hastily withdrew the proposal. Bad move.

Parking meter

Oklahoma City introduced the first parking meter, which came into service on 16 July 1935. It was one of a initial batch of 150 Park-O-Meters ordered from the Dual Parking Meter Company, also of Oklahoma City. Now practically every city in the world uses parking meters, some mechanical, some electronic, some using coins, some using cards. They are highly valued by municipalities because they produce considerable revenue as well as regulating parking on the streets.

Oklahoma City's first parking meters came about through the rather dubious activities of the Businessmen's Traffic Committee, which was set up in 1933 to impose stricter parking controls on the city streets. The Committee's Chairman was Carlton Magee, editor of a local newspaper. With no apparent concession to the notion of conflicting interests, Magee established the Dual Parking Meter Company, so called because it was charged with coming up with devices that both regulated parking and generated revenue for the city. The company unsurprisingly won the contract to provide the meters.

Parking meters first started springing up on the streets of Britain in 1958. They were American imports at first and then home grown in the 1960s. With them came the dreaded parking wardens, or 'meter maids' as they came to be known. The ironic serenade 'Lovely Rita' (meter maid) was released by The Beatles on their Sergeant Pepper's Lonely Hearts Club Band album in 1967, and it inspired David Bailey's photograph for The Beatles Illustrated Lyrics edited by Alan Aldridge and published in 1969. By the end of the 1990s there were signs that the parking meter's time was up in Britain as pay-and-display machines began to take over. In Birmingham today there is not a parking meter to be found.

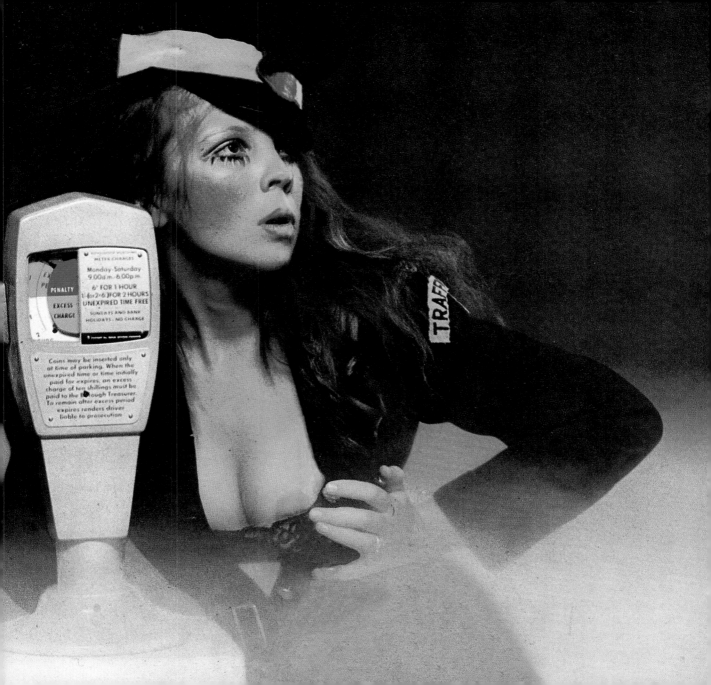

Catseyes road stud

Percy Shaw, a Yorkshire businessman, noticed that drivers at night often relied on the reflection of their headlights in tramlines to guide them. This gave him the idea of devising a purpose-built road reflector. Shaw filed a patent for his invention in 1934 and formed Reflecting Roadstuds Limited in Halifax, Yorkshire on 15 March 1935. Ministry of Transport tests on competing devices proved Shaw's design to be the best. Business boomed after the war and by the 1990s sales had passed 16 million.

'Catseyes' studs derived their name from two small mirrors with round lenses in each stud which point towards on-coming traffic. Placed at intervals along lane lines or roadsides the studs reflect the headlights of vehicles at night, thereby marking the lanes and edges of the road for drivers.

Shaw's stroke of genius was to make the stud so that it depressed into its housing on a rubber mounting when a wheel went over it. When it popped up again the movement had cleaned the lenses of the Catseyes so that they always remained bright, giving maximum reflection with no maintenance.

Percy Shaw, inventor of Catseyes reflecting road studs, was paid a royalty on every one sold, which allowed him to enjoy his retirement comfortably.

Suntan lotion

Until the start of the 1930s, lily-white skin had long been fashionable among the well-to-do. Coco Chanel changed all that when she appeared in 1925 with a suntan, creating a fashion sensation. Although all kinds of expensive salves, creams, lotions and oils were used to protect the skin and promote the tans of the new generation of sunbathers, it was only in 1936 that L'Oréal brought out the first mass-market sun lotion, called Ambre Solaire.

Coco Chanel, the legendary fashion designer who gave the world the little black dress and Chanel No. 5, had bought a house in the South of France, where she allowed the sun to darken her skin. Such was the power of Chanel that a fashion craze for suntanned skin was born.

By the 1990s the tanned look was under attack from doctors. With holes appearing in the ozone layer, letting in more ultraviolet light, exposure to sun increased the likelihood of skin cancer. Reluctant to give up the tanned look, people simply used more and more suntan cream and oil.

Coco Chanel revolutionized women's fashion in the 1920s with the chemise dress and collarless cardigan jacket. She retired in 1938, made a comeback in 1954 and died in 1971.

Overleaf: *August in Paris and the remaining population who haven't gone away on holiday spread themselves in the sun at a public swimming pool to change the colour of their skins.*

Supermarket trolley/cart

On 4 June 1937 Sylvan Goldman, manager of the Humpty Dumpty supermarket in Oklahoma City, introduced the first supermarket trolleys to his shoppers. The idea was a hit and the supermarket trolley has become second only to the motor car as the world's most frequently used four-wheeled vehicle.

Business was bad in 1936 and Sylvan Goldman was looking for ways to improve his trade. He noticed that his women customers were coming into the store carrying their own baskets, only to stop shopping when they were full. This gave him the idea of a shopping basket on wheels to allow customers to buy at least twice as much and not have to carry it.

The first Humpty Dumpty supermarket trolley was made by local handyman Fred Young who used a metal folding chair, added wheels to the legs and fitted two baskets, one above the other. Goldman placed several of these new trolleys by the door of the store and hired people to push the trolleys filled with groceries around the store. It clicked.

For one homeless unfortunate in San Francisco a supermarket trolley carries all her worldly goods. Towards the end of the century there were still a great many others like her on the streets of the world's richest cities.

This cover for the July 1958 issue of Esquire magazine lampoons the American obsession with anything instant or convenient which lay behind the huge success of instant coffee. It was art directed by Henry Wolf, who was with the magazine between 1952 and 1958. He was perhaps the greatest of the post-war New York art directors, and his work was always expressive with a surrealistic tendency to surprise. He went on to Harper's Bazaar, and then Show magazine in 1961.

Instant coffee

Instant coffee was invented in the spring of 1937 following eight years of research by Nestlé in Switzerland; it was launched in 1938 under the name of Nescafé. After the interruption of the war, it became hugely popular on both sides of the Atlantic. Although much derided by purists, it appealed to an age obsessed by convenience.

The task of reducing coffee beans to a soluble powder had been undertaken by the company following suggestions made by the Brazilian Institute of Coffee in 1930.

The freeze-drying process that Nestlé developed eliminates only the water, while retaining the volatile oils of coffee essential to the taste. This is achieved by driving off the water while it is frozen under vacuum conditions. The process was also turned to tea and other foods, and 'instant' became the one of the favourite catchwords of the ad men. Most of these other products had brief lives, but instant coffee endured, becoming a beverage in its own right and often found alongside real coffee in the larder or fridge.

The British and the Japanese like instant coffee the best. By the mid-1990s in a market valued at £705 million, over 70 million cups of instant were being drunk in Britain every day, which is around 90 per cent of all coffee consumed.

Suspending the 1 million square foot (100,000 sq m) Teflon-coated canopy for the Millennium Dome in Greenwich, London.

Teflon

While the American chemical company Du Pont was busy inventing nylon and telling the world about it in the late 1930s, it was also keeping absolutely quiet about another material that one of its scientists had stumbled on. This was Teflon, so extraordinary that its discovery had to be accidental. It was an inert substance, completely stable – corrosion proof, unaffected by heat, electricity, acids and solvents. It also had the lowest coefficient of friction of any substance known to man. In other words, it was slippery – more slippery than wet ice on wet ice.

Du Pont's Jackson Laboratory in New Jersey was the scene. Roy Plunkett was the man. His project was to find a non-toxic gas for use in refrigerator compressors. On 6 April 1938 a lab assistant called Jack Rebok opened a gas cylinder of freon (tetrafluoroethylene) that Plunkett had made – but no gas came out. The two men thought it must have leaked, but when they weighed the cylinder they found that it was still full. They sawed it in half and saw a greasy white power. What had happened was that the molecules

The New York Times Magazine

FEBRUARY 22,1976/SECTION 6

LOOKING AT: RONALD REAGAN

Shoot-out in New Hampshire

CONTENTS: PAGE 4

Ronald Regan became known as the 'Teflon President' because no matter what accusations of scandal or impropriety were thrown at him they never stuck. This cover image was specially created by Fluck and Law, the Spitting Image puppet makers.

of the gas Plunkett had thought he was making had formed into long chains. He had inadvertently invented a polymer – one the very first plastics.

Teflon's amazing properties soon came to the attention of the military, and during the war it became a closely guarded secret. It was used in the Manhattan Project as the only material capable of resisting the corrosive uranium hexafluoride, which was used in making uranium-235, the fissile material of the first atom bomb.

Teflon's existence was made public in 1946, and its civil development began. Today Teflon is perhaps best known as the coating on non-stick pans. It was in fact the French who first introduced this use, in May 1956. Teflon pots and pans were launched in America in 1960 but initially gained a poor reputation because the material was so non-stick it wouldn't bond properly to the metal backing and came off too easily. (The problem has since been fixed.)

However it is Teflon's industrial and scientific uses that make it such a profoundly important material. In medicine Teflon is so inert that the body does not reject it, making it ideal for artificial blood vessels and bone joints. In electronics it is widely used as cable insulation. Teflon went into space as a coating for the space suit of John Glenn, the first American to orbit the earth, and has since ridden to the moon, Mars, Jupiter, and beyond the solar system.

It is also widely used in bridges and buildings, as it is weather-resistant and flame retardant. Even the Statue of Liberty now has Teflon coatings and spacers to insulate the copper skin from the steel frame, thus preventing corrosion. And Teflon is there to mark the end of the century and the start of the new millennium in the roof skin of London's huge Millennium Dome.

Ballpoint pen

It was in the 1930s that the Hungarian Ladislao José Biró, editor of a well-known magazine in Budapest, became fascinated with other uses for the quick-drying ink used by his printers. This led him to the idea for a pen with quick-drying ink fed by capillary action to a rolling ball nib, and he patented the idea in 1938.

In 1940 Biró went to Argentina to escape the Nazis and in 1944 he sold out to his English backer H. G. Martin, who began marketing the 'Biro' pens in the UK for £2 15s. They were made by the Miles Martin Pen Co. in a disused aircraft hangar near Reading, Berkshire and production in the first year reached 30,000 pens. The Biro was introduced to the USA at a New York department store and 10,000 were sold at $12.50 each on the very first day.

In 1958 Biró's original patent for the ballpoint pen was taken over by the Frenchman Marcel Bich. He had the great idea to create a disposable version of the ballpoint pen, which he called the Bic. Eventually the idea took off and by the 1990s three billion Bics a year were being sold around the world.

An ingenious demonstration of the ballpoint's endurance was created by the Swiss designer Ruedi Külling in this graphic device for Bic. The image was originally used for a 1968 poster advertising campaign in Switzerland.

BiC Kugelschreiber

First Step, 1966, by Allen Jones. A painter and printmaker, Jones is also well known for his sculptures of women which double as pieces of furniture. He first made his mark in 1961 at the Young Contemporaries exhibition and he was the designer for the costumes and the sets of the nude review Oh Calcutta! in 1969. He remains one of Britain's most committed Pop artists, and the consistently erotic tone of his imagery has predictably landed him in some trouble with the more puritanical adherents of political correctness.

Nylon stockings

The first nylon stockings went on sale in the USA on 15 May 1940, and four million pairs sold out in four days. Nylon was the world's first synthetic fibre and had been patented in 1937 by Dr Wallace H. Corothers, leader of a research team at the chemical company E. I. du Pont de Nemours, now known as Du Pont.

When hemlines went up in the 1920s to reveal the legs of women for the first time in centuries, if not millennia, stockings became an essential fashion item. Flesh coloured hosiery gave the impression of bare legs while masking the odd blemish and bulge.

By the end of the 1930s, word got out about a new wonder fibre that would give stockings the resilience as well as the look and feel that women had been waiting for. The new stockings, known simply as 'nylons', were to become a fashion sensation.

Commercial production of nylon had begun at Du Pont's New Jersey plant in 1938 and found its first use in the bristles of toothbrushes. In 1939, the company started making nylon yarn for stockings in Delaware. The name 'nylon' was reputedly inspired by the cities it was thought would give it the greatest marketing cachet – New York and London.

When America entered the war in 1941, the production of stockings practically stopped. Their rarity gave them a new role as a kind of barter currency with GIs in Europe.

In 1945 nylons began to return to the shops in America. In New York, Macy's stock of 50,000 pairs sold out in six hours. British-made nylon stockings went on sale for the first time in 1946.

When the Second World War caused a nylon famine, eye liner drawn up the backs of bare legs to make faux seams created the illusion of wearing stockings.

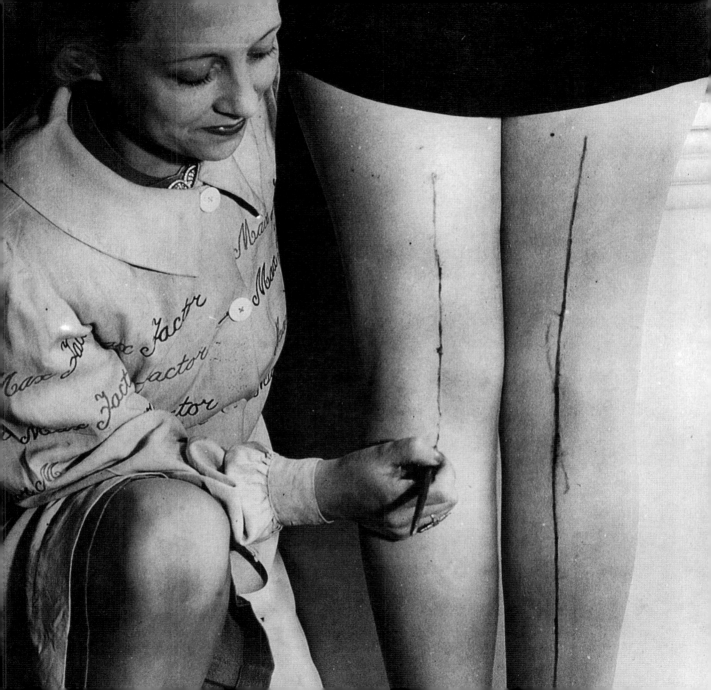

T-shirt

In 1942 the US Navy issued the specification for its new 'T-type' undershirt. It was to be made out of white cotton, with a round neck and short sleeves at right angles to the body, making a 'T'. It soon began to be called the T-shirt, and US Navy and Marine personnel liked it so much they began to wear it as a shirt in its own right – not least because of the effect it had on girls. By the end of the war T-shirts with unit or division names printed on the chest began to appear. The modern T-shirt phenomenon had started.

T-shirt protest: the Campaign for Nuclear Disarmament (CND) symbol designed by Gerald Holtom first appeared in 1958.

White cotton vests with short sleeves in various forms had been worn well before the turn of the century. But it was the particular style of the new T-shirt that set it apart. In the years after the war, demobbed military personnel continued to wear their T-shirts and they began to be made commercially.

In the 1950s the new breed of stars such as Marlon Brando and James Dean appeared in their in early, defining films – and they wore T-shirts. The style had to be adopted by the young and fashionable, who liked to think of themselves as rebels too. As cheaper and better techniques were developed, the printing of T-shirts became a big industry. The printed T-shirt seemed to appeal to everybody: bearing an emblem became a statement of individualism; carrying the name and colours of a team or a college declared a sense of belonging.

In the 1960s, when self-expression reached new heights, the T-shirt bore ever more avant-garde images, from the psychedelic insignia of rock bands to ban-the-bomb symbols and other

Marlon Brando, the first big star from Lee Strasberg's Actors' Studio in New York, with its emphasis on 'method' acting, in the 1951 screen version of Tennessee Williams's A Streetcar Named Desire. *Brando went on to depict the original motorbike rebel in* The Wild One *in 1953 and won an Oscar for* On the Waterfront *in 1954. He won another for* The Godfather *in 1972, but turned it down in protest at the film industry's treatment of the American Indian.*

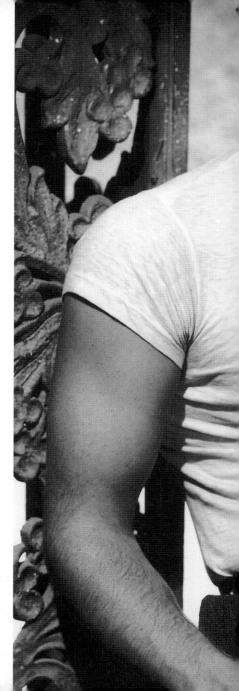

propaganda. The idea of the T-shirt as a personal advertising hoarding was not lost on the marketing men, who discovered that people would willingly promote their interests for free. Cheap to make, big brands only need the lightest excuse to give away T-shirts blazoning their logos and slogans.

Soft toilet paper

In 1942 the British experienced for the first time something that gave them a great deal of comfort. Until then they had endured rough and not very absorbent single-ply impregnated paper in the toilet, which they took to be the norm. All that changed with the launch of Andrex soft toilet paper rolls, first made at St Andrew's Paper Mill in Walthamstow, London.
In America early in the century consumers wouldn't discuss toilet paper, merchants wouldn't display it and publications wouldn't advertise it. So manufacturers had to supply toilet paper under the names of the drug stores selling it. In 1955 Scott Paper was the first to advertise toilet paper on television. In Britain the first of many Andrex commercials went out in 1972 with a puppy running about the place with an unravelling toilet roll.

Overleaf: Napoli football fans in the San Paolo Stadium applaud their team by bombarding the pitch with streaming rolls of toilet paper.

Bikini

The US government unwittingly set in motion the train of events that resulted in the bikini. In attempting to eliminate textile wastage during the Second World War, it reduced by one-tenth the amount of fabric allowed for women's swimwear. Designers responded and made the required cuts by simply taking out the midriff of the one-piece swimsuit, and the two-piece swimsuit was born.

Soon after the end of the war, the Frenchman Jacques Heim developed the American two-piece swimsuit into what he called the Atome, because of its tiny size. In 1946 he introduced it for sale in his beach shop at Cannes. On 5 July that same year, rival French couturier Louis Réard introduced his two-piece swimsuit at a Paris poolside fashion show. He thought the creation so explosively sensational (and with some reference to Heim's Atome) that he named it after the Bikini Atoll in the South Pacific, where the USA had just tested an atom bomb.

Supermodels in the 1990s will wear practically anything or nothing to grab the headlines for fashion designers – and themselves. In 1946 it was quite a different matter and the prevailing attitudes towards decency meant that none of the professional catwalk models would wear Réard's creation for its first public showing. So he went out and enlisted the help of a dancer at the Casino in Paris. Her name was

Micheline Bernardi and the image of her reclining in the new bikini brought her instant fame when it was flashed around the world.

It took a few years, but by the mid-1950s film stars began to wear bikinis, causing a stir to begin with, but gradually with less and less fuss. By 1960 the bikini's acceptability was confirmed with a 'seal of approval' from *Harper's Bazaar* magazine, and by that summer's mainstream pop hit, 'Yellow Polka Dot Bikini' by one Brian Hyland. The bikini held sway for a decade until 1970 when, a beach at St Tropez just along from Cannes where it had all started, women began to discard the top half of their bikinis, and a new kind of one-piece swimsuit was born.

After appearing on the cover of Elle magazine at the age of 15, Brigitte Bardot fatefully met and married French film director Roger Vadim. In 1953 Vadim 'unveiled' Bardot at the Cannes Film Festival where in a bikini she stole the limelight from established stars who had to pose with her to get their pictures taken (in this case Kirk Douglas and Denise de Lenthec). In 1956 she appeared in Vadim's Et Dieu créa la femme (And God Created Woman). Initially banned in America and elsewhere, the film single-handedly liberalized the cinema with its hitherto unimagined sensuality. As the original 'sex kitten' Bardot, or Bébé as she became known, led women into a new era where they ceased to take the cue for their sexuality from men. After a super-star career which lasted through the 1960s, Bardot gradually went into retreat, became reclusive and took up the cause of animal rights.

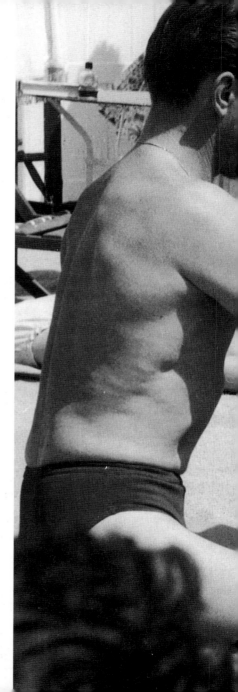

Espresso machine

In 1938 Italian designer and engineer Achille Gaggia invented a piston system for forcing hot water at high pressure through finely ground coffee contained in a filtered holder. After the Second World War, Gaggia's first commercial espresso machine was introduced in 1946.

Italians quickly took to the wake-up effect of a nip of black coffee so strong it was almost like hot coffee juice. Espresso bars began to appear at railway stations and street corners.

Enterprising caterers began to use espresso as the basis for various preparations with different forms of milk and cream, producing coffee favourites like mocha and cappuccino. As the Gaggia machines reached other countries their output was adapted to suit local tastes. By the 1990s 35 per cent of all espresso machines were still made by Gaggia, whose original design has been adapted to a wide range of models suiting anything from large-scale catering operations to domestic kitchens.

In the late 1950s English teenagers flocked to the new Gaggia-equipped coffee bars. One of the most famous was the '2 Is' in Soho where Bermondsey boy Tommy Steele played the first British rock. The coffee-bar scene was satirized in the 1959 film Expresso Bongo, starring the young Cliff Richard.

atom

The terror of the

age

is not the violence of the new power
but the speed of man's adjustment to it
– the speed of his acceptance.

E. B. White

Credit card

The forerunner of the modern credit card was the Charg-It system launched by the Flatbush National Bank, New York, in 1946. This combined consumer credit with a cashless method of payment. The BankAmericard was then launched in California in 1959. It expanded to other states in 1966 and was renamed Visa in 1976/77. Mastercard soon followed, with Barclaycard introduced in the UK in 1966. The proliferation of cards towards the end of the century is linked to the growing investment by banks in electronic systems for payment transfers.

Credit cards, which have a specified credit limit and charge interest on accounts not paid off, are descended from payment cards, which were introduced in the USA in the 1920s, initially by service stations and hotels and soon after by shops. They became known as 'shoppers' plates' and only used in the retail and service outlets that issued them.

The shoppers' plate was similar to the modern charge card, which differs from the credit card in that it requires the full account to be settled every month. The cost of credit cards is met by interest charges, while charge cards have no interest charges but carry an annual fee. The first universal charge card, Diners Club, was introduced in 1950 and was followed by American Express in 1958.

The vulnerability of credit and charge cards to misuse has led to the application of ever more sophisticated security technology on the card itself, first with its electronic strip and latterly with its holographic anti-forging mark — measures that have been relatively successful in deterring and preventing fraud. But fraud is not the only unauthorized use that the card is subject to. A well-known trick that is used to open a door with a rim lock is to slip a credit card into the crack and ease back the bolt. It works better in movies than in reality.

Polaroid camera

The Polaroid Corporation was founded in 1937 by Edwin H. Land at the age of 28, originally to specialize in sunglasses and polarizing filters. In 1943 Land conceived of the idea for an instant camera when he took a photograph of his daughter; she asked why she couldn't see the picture straight away. In 1946 the first test Polaroid picture was taken – a view of Harvard Yard in Cambridge, Massachusetts. Two years later the company launched the Polaroid 95, the world's first instant picture camera.

Polaroid's first 'brown'-and-white film took over a minute to develop. But as the unique developing emulsions were improved the image appeared more quickly, the tear-off covering paper was eliminated and in 1963 the first Polaroid colour film was introduced.

Edwin Land was a great accumulator of patents. The year before the

David Hockney, certainly the best known and perhaps the greatest of Britain's post-war artists, had already achieved international success by his mid-20s. His first one-man show in London was held in 1963 when he was 26 and his first retrospective as early as 1970. The many paintings he has produced featuring swimming pools are in some ways a celebration of his love affair with Los Angeles. His Polaroid composite, Ian Swimming, was made in 1982.

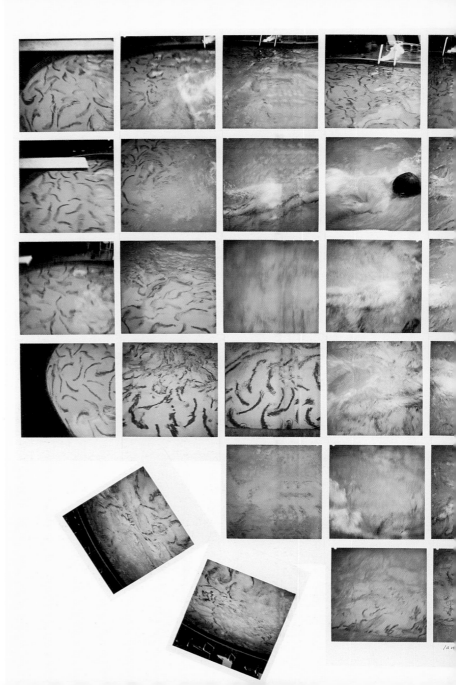

114

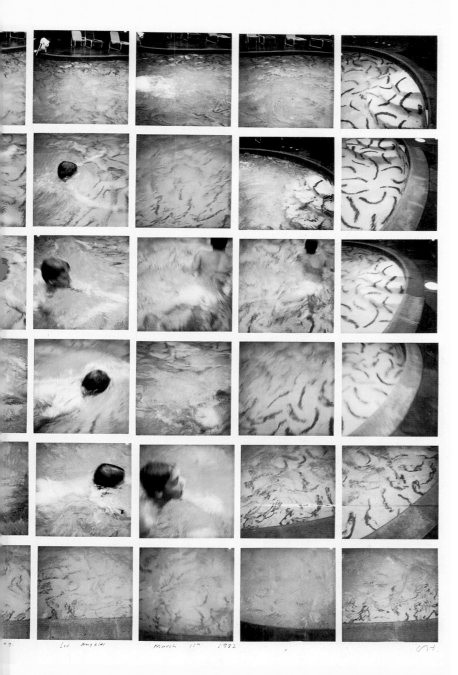

launch of the first Polaroid camera, Kodak got to hear of the idea but showed no interest in developing its own version. But by 1976 Polaroid's success had led Kodak to introduce a rival instant picture camera. Polaroid sued for patent infringement and judgement was made in its favour. Polaroid were given back exclusive rights to the process and awarded $1 billion damages.

Electric guitar

Microphones had been attached to guitars in various makeshift ways since the 1920s, when blues singers and jazzmen began experimenting with the new sounds that came from amplifying their instruments. The earliest is attributed to the American Lloyd Loar. In 1935 a more sophisticated instrument was designed by Adolph Rickenbacher, whose Electric Vibrola Spanish Guitar was made out of Bakelite and had a special microphone on the back. The first true electric guitar with direct amplification of the strings was made by Paul Bigsby in 1947.

It was guitarist Merle Travis who had commissioned Paul Bigsby's innovation, and the early development of electric guitars tended to be driven by the demands of musicians. In 1948, Leo Fender produced his first electric guitar, called the Broadcaster, with the Telecaster following in 1950. The legendary Fender Stratocaster designed by Fred Tavaras appeared in 1954.

The arrival of the Stratocaster gave impetus to a new form of music that was also just beginning in 1954: rock 'n' roll. Already the sounds of the urban bluesmen from Chicago and Detroit had defined the new ways of playing when the guitar was amplified. This began to influence the sound of rock and, eventually, practically all forms of youth-oriented pop.

The electric guitar made heroes of its proponents, not simply by the sound that was produced, but by the manner in which it was played on stage. Plugged or unplugged, the guitar held like a tommy-gun became a powerful symbol of sexuality. Led by the extraordinary 1950s performances of Elvis Presley, singers quickly realized that they did not have to be guitar virtuosos to use the instrument to effect.

In the 1960s and early 1970s blues-based guitarists such as Eric Clapton and Jimi Hendrix (who did know how to play), took the instrument on to a new plane. They defined the appearance and approach of most rock artists as well as the music itself, with its variety of offspring, for the rest of the century.

Eric Clapton established himself as one of the leading exponents of the white blues guitar in the 1960s with the seminal British group The Yardbirds. He went on to play in a number of 'supergroups' including Derek and the Dominos and Cream in the late 1960s and early 1970s. Adopting a gentler style later on in his career has endeared him to an even wider audience and his annual London concerts in the 1990s continue to sell out.

Aluminium foil

Aluminium foil in easy-to-handle rolls for use in the kitchen for cooking and wrapping food was introduced in 1947 by the Reynolds Metals Co. in the USA. Until the advent of aluminium, metal foil had been the exclusive province of tin, and in Britain, where aluminium foil was first introduced in 1962, it is still colloquially referred to as tin foil.

The commercial extraction of aluminium from alumina was achieved in America and France independently towards the end of the 19th century. Aluminium made its first entry into the kitchen in the form of the kettle. Other cookware, auto components, electric wire and cable were soon being made in the novel metal. In 1903 the Wright Brothers' *Flyer 1* made the world's first powered flight using aluminium parts. By 1912 aluminium had taken over from tin as the material used for thin-sheet 'foil' and was used by industry and in an increasing number of consumer products such as the tops of milk bottles.

The idea for using it as a food wrap for cooking had come from a Reynolds executive before the Second World War. When his wife found that she did

Aluminium foil being used in a new perm technique devised by Parisian coiffeur Patrick Ales. The foil prevents the hair from being dried out by the perming tongs and thus gives longer-lasting and more regular waves.

not have a roasting pan for the Thanksgiving turkey, he suggested she use some aluminium foil that he had in his briefcase to show to some commercial kitchen customers. America had to wait until peacetime to start roasting their turkeys in Reynolds Wrap. Today aluminium foil is found in 98 per cent of all American kitchens.

False eyelashes

David and Eric Aylott were film studio make-up artists working in the 1940s and 1950s with such screen goddesses as Elizabeth Taylor and Sophia Loren. Eyes have always been given special emphasis in preparing for the big screen, and in 1947 the brothers successfully developed false eyelash strips to enhance the flutter and accentuate the effect of this most expressive part of a movie star's face. Ever intent on emulating the style of the stars, movie-goers began to demand false eyelashes for themselves. So the Aylotts launched a consumer version called Eylure, a ready-to-wear strip. When the radical new look of the 1960s demanded heavily made-up eyes, preferably with false eyelashes, Eylure began selling at the rate of eight million pairs a year.

Eric Aylott went on to create false fingernails. These also became a popular accessory that allowed working women to have conveniently short nails during the day and to adopt the elegantly long nails of the idle rich in the evening.

Being the adventures of a yo whose principal interests a ultra-violence and Beeth

STANLEY KUBR

CLOCKWOR ORANGE

A Stanley Kubrick Production "A CLOCKWORK ORANGE" Starring Malcolm McDowel Patrick Magee · Adrienne Corri and Miriam Karlin · Screenplay by Stanley Kubrick Based on the novel by Anthony Burgess · Produced and Directed by Stanley Kubrick Executive Producers Max L. Raab and Si Litvinoff · **From Warner Bros** Ⓦ **A Warner Communications Company** Released by Columbia-Warner Distributors Ltd · Original Soundtrack recording on Warner Bros. K46127

man
ape,
n.

K'S

PRINTED IN ENGLAND BY W E BERRY LTD BRADFORD

Heavy eye make-up and false eyelashes were used to accentuate menace in A Clockwork Orange. The lead character, played by Malcolm McDowell, is here depicted in Philip Castle's poster for Stanley Kubrick's notorious 1971 film. Based on the Anthony Burgess novel, it concerns the exploits of a young man who chooses to express himself in violence. The director was so concerned about the publicity generated by the film, which he felt might have a corrupting affect on certain elements of British youth, that he withdrew it from distribution in Britain.

Microwave oven

In late 1946 the Raytheon Company in the USA filed a patent that showed how microwaves could be used for cooking food. A prototype microwave oven was made and installed in a Boston restaurant for testing. The first commercial models came on to the market in 1947. They stood five and a half feet (1.6 m) tall and weighed over 750 pounds (350 kg). The magnetron tube inside which made the whole thing possible had to be water cooled, and the new type of oven cost $5,000.

The magic of the microwave oven stemmed directly from the development of radar by Britain during the Second World War. By bombarding whatever has to be cooked with very high frequency electromagnetic waves (microwaves) the molecules of the food vibrate and heat up. The microwaves are generated by an electron tube called a magnetron, which was invented in 1940 by John Randall and H. A. H. Boot, who were working on ways to improve radar systems so that they could be carried in aircraft. (John Randall later went on to oversee crucial work on the discovery of DNA at King's College London in the 1950s.)

Naturally the invention was given to the Americans, as wartime allies, and President Roosevelt described the arrival of the magnetron as 'the most valuable cargo ever to reach our shores'. The magnetron became the

heart of radar, which was used decisively by British anti-aircraft gunners, fighters and night bombers and was important in destroying U-boats in the Battle of the Atlantic. It is notable that early radar engineers are said to have tested whether their magnetron was working by sticking their fingers near it to see if they warmed up.

After the war, Raytheon engineer Dr Percy Spencer was working with a magnetron in radar-related research. He also noticed how it warmed up things. He put some popcorn kernels near the tube and watched them pop all over the laboratory. He tried an egg, which exploded spectacularly. Spencer then put together the first makeshift microwave oven, consisting of a metal box into which he fed the microwave output of the magnetron.

It took a while for the market and manufacturers to work out what microwave ovens were good for – and what they weren't good for. By 1976 microwaves ovens were to be found in nearly 60 per cent of American homes and were outselling gas cookers.

One of the differences between cooking with microwaves and conventional ovens is that the microwaves generate heat evenly right through the food, while the oven applies heat to the outside so that it gradually works its way in. The story goes that one lady who had bought a microwave did not understand this principle and thought it was some kind of fan oven because of the noise it made. So, after shampooing her poodle, she put it into the microwave to dry off ...

TV chat show

The origins of the television talk show can be traced to a 1948 musical revue on NBC in the USA called _Garroway at Large,_ in which the host Dave Garroway chatted informally to guest singers and musicians in the studio. The format was established with a variety of talk shows over the following ten years or so featuring hosts such as Edward R. Morrow and Jack Paar chatting to a succession of guests, usually well-known.

In the early 1960s the American networks took over from sponsors and advertisers as the main generators of talk shows and launched a new breed of hosts – Johnny Carson, Barbara Walters and Mike Wallace – who became national stars. In the 1970s Phil Donahue pioneered the audience-participation talk show that has proved to be even more popular than the original format. It has been taken to new heights, or depths, by Oprah Winfrey, whose show began in 1986, and now the _Jerry Springer Show,_ which has become number one with viewers in the USA.

The world's longest running talk show is the _Late Late Show_ hosted by Gay Byrne on Ireland's RTE 1. It started on 6 July 1962, with just eight shows scheduled, and is still going strong. Gay Byrne's show is also unique in being two hours long and it has remained in Ireland's top ratings ever since its first showings.

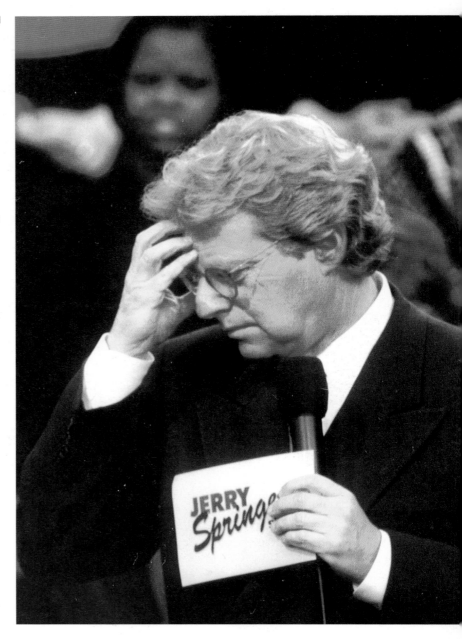

Notorious for its racy topics and the tears and tantrums of the participating audience, the Jerry Springer Show bases its success on viewers' voyeuristic fascination with appalling attitudes and behaviour exhibited by ordinary people. In 1998 it overtook the Oprah Winfrey Show as America's favourite. Springer had been Cincinnati's Mayor in 1977 and received seven Emmy Awards for his nightly commentaries on Cincinnati television.

Parkinson was the BBC's most successful talk show and ran between 1971 and 1982, returning for a nostalgic series in 1998. Talk was something that Muhammed Ali was also good at and he won his verbal sparring match with Michael Parkinson in 1971, and again in the return match in 1974. Certainly the greatest boxer, some say the greatest sportsman, of all time, the 'Louisville Lip' was three times heavyweight champion and at one point

arguably the most famous man in the world. As Cassius Clay he won an Olympic gold medal in 1960 and his first heavyweight championship against Sonny Liston in 1964. He became a Muslim, refused military service and was stripped of his title in 1967. He returned to the ring in 1970 and his fights with Joe Frazier in 1971 and 1974 and George Foreman in 1978 were among the most extraordinary the sport has seen.

Photo: David Bailey

It takes up to 40 dumb animals to make a fur c

If you don't want animals gassed, electrocuted, trapped or strangled, don't buy a fur

But only one to wear it.

🐾 respect for animals

PO Box 500, Nottingham NG1 3AS

Fake fur

George Borg of Borg Warner, the automotive components company, bought the Bradley Knitting Mills in Wisconsin from a friend in 1947. He discovered a machine there which made polishing discs out of circles of fabric for use on cars as they came off the assembly line. In 1948 Borg adapted the idea with a method for introducing fibres to the needle to give the fabric a deep pile – the basis for fake fur. Du Pont's synthetic Orlon fibre was used for the fibre and the resultant 'seal' fabric became the hallmark of what came to be known simply as 'Borg', the generic name for fake fur.

Borg set up his fake-fur business with plants in Wisconsin, expanded to Georgia and Connecticut and then overseas to Britain, Belgium and Canada. The burgeoning animal-rights movements of the 1960s and 1970s began to embarrass people wearing the fur of animals killed for the purpose, and fake fur became increasingly fashionable. In 1970 a method for making non-geometric patterns which led to the 'leopard-look' was invented and further developed for Borg in France. Computer-aided design and manufacture now allows fake-fur-weaving machines to copy the film image of a pattern however complicated.

David Bailey took the photograph for the anti-fur coat campaign poster which first appeared on hoardings in Britain in 1986.

Emulsion/latex paint

A two-page advertisement in *Life* magazine appeared in 1949 proclaiming 'A new Wonder Paint almost beyond belief'. This was the launch of Spred Satin, and the beginning of a revolution that redefined the paint industry. Known as latex in America and emulsion in Britain, the new paint was made by the Glidden Co. In the first year 100,000 gallons (450,000 litres) were sold, reaching 3.5 million gallons (15.75 million litres) two years later.

Glidden had spent decades researching alternatives for petroleum solvents in paints before the Second World War. After building a soybean-oil extraction plant in Chicago in 1934, it adopted a German process under licence to produce lecithin, a soybean-oil by-product used in paint as well as many other things such as margarine, rubber and sweets. By the mid-1940s Glidden had developed a full line of soy-protein and water-based paints.

Yves Klein, the French experimental artist, was a showman as much as he was a painter and he caused an outcry when he opened his show 'Le Vide' at a Paris gallery in 1958: the gallery was empty. For his Anthropométries, 1960, he used blue emulsion paint and three models, performing for 40 minutes to a string ensemble in front of 100 invited guests, to create imprints of the human body. Klein died two years later at the age of 34.

The breakthrough was the invention of water-borne latex paint, which reduced the petroleum-based solvent content by about 90 per cent. For users, latex or emulsion paint was a boon. Brushes and rollers could be cleaned under the tap rather than with expensive white spirit or turpentine. The paint went on smoothly and easily and its covering power was excellent.

Glidden was acquired in 1986 by British chemical giant ICI, owner of the Dulux brand and market leader for emulsion paint in Britain and Europe. Spred Satin continues to be a leading brand in the USA, where 75 per cent of all paint sales were latex by the 1990s.

Training shoes/ sneakers

Modern training shoes can be traced back to the Three Stripes running shoe design which was registered in Germany by Adolf 'Adi' Dassler in 1949. Brothers Adolf and Rudolf Dassler had started making soccer boots and spiked track shoes before the Second World War. Olympic athletes at the 1928 Games wore Dassler shoes, as did Jesse Owens for his triumph at the Berlin Games in 1936. In 1948 the brothers split up and Adolf started Addas, later to be called Adidas, while Rudolf founded the Puma brand.

The training-shoe phenomenon grew out of the general liberalization of attitudes to dressing and the increasing interest in physical fitness in the second half of the century. In the 1970s, shoes designed to serve the needs of athletic activity began to enter the world of fashion. By the end of the century, training shoes had joined blue jeans as universally 'democratic' wear for all ages and all nationalities.

When the keep-fit movement began in the 1970s and surged in the 1980s, gyms and fitness centres opened and urban parks filled with panting and plodding joggers. Yet training shoes became big business not simply because everyone was running around and jumping up and down in the evenings and on weekends but because they were comfortable and made you look fit even if you never raised a sweat.

Training shoes took on cult status among the young and manufacturers traded on the minute style changes and embellishments that gave the shoes very special status to aficionados. It is said that gangs of inner city kids in the USA would even kill for them. By the 1990s the giant manufacturers were bidding billions in their efforts to gain advantage for their brand names at the great world sporting occasions such as the Olympic Games and World Cup.

During the transit strike of 1980, New Yorkers were forced to walk miles from Brooklyn or Queens to get to work in Manhattan. They took to their sneakers to make the trek more tolerable and soon the sight of suited executives with such incongruous footwear became commonplace, which had as much to do with making fashion statements as comfort.

Hairspray

When the American company Kiquinet Corp. introduced the first aerosol hairspray in 1949 it immediately had a huge impact on the hair-care habits of women. Without having to visit the hairdresser, hair could be kept in place all day long with a spray of lacquer first thing. In 1952, 25 million aerosol hairspray cans were sold. In 1953, hairsprays became the leading seller in the market for beauty and personal products, which included deodorants, suntan creams, perfumes and shampoos.

Shellac was the first fixative polymer used in aerosols (see also Aerosol, page 63). It was readily available at the time and, bleached and dewaxed, it provided high sheen, good holding ability and resisted the weather well. However, it was difficult to brush through and, not being soluble in water, did not wash out easily. Also, because the solvent used was highly flammable alcohol, the aerosol had an alarming tendency to turn into a blow-torch if the woman were smoking while fixing her hair.

New formulations were tried in the late 1950s, and the synthetic PVP was introduced which proved to be more reliable and was soluble in water. Further formulation advances were made in the 1970s and 1980s allowing the highly structured hairstyles which have become popular in the latter part of the century.

Her fashionable beehive style only possible because of hair spray, Mandy Rice-Davies was in trouble with the law in 1963 as one of the girls in the revelations of the 'Profumo Affair', which at one time threatened to bring down Harold Macmillan's Government. The other girl was her friend Christine Keeler, with whom cabinet minister John Profumo compromised himself — and national security.

Domestic rubber gloves

Latex rubber gloves designed for domestic use were introduced in 1950 by the J. Allen Rubber Company, a small Gloucestershire concern that had been making babies' bottle teats and soothers since the 1930s. The first Marigold gloves were orange and were sold in chemist's shops in a range of sizes and two finishes, smooth and crêpe. They were expensive, and were considered luxury items.

Stiff rubber gloves on a leather lining had been made by Thomas Hancock, the English rubber pioneer who introduced many kinds of products such as garters, braces, straps and kneecaps, in the mid-19th century. But his gloves were only suitable for heavy industrial use.

At the beginning of the 20th century Edwardian women began to discard the dress gloves habitually worn by Victorians and so became more sensitive about the state of their hands. During and after the First World War domestic staff became rarer and more women turned to housework. The consequent reddening and chapping of hands were not helped by the chemicals in the new soaps and detergents.

Still no material with the right supple, waterproof and perish-resistant qualities was available for gloves to protect housewives' hands, and the application of skin creams remained the only answer. Finally latex rubber

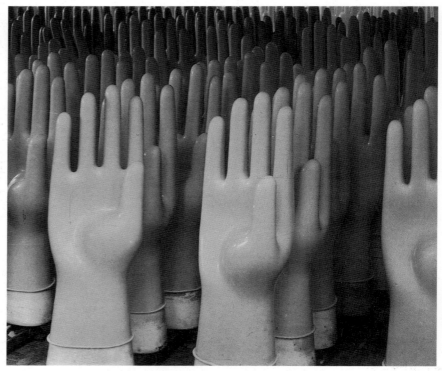

technology had advanced sufficiently during and after the Second World War to fulfil the long-held desire of so many women for effective and comfortable household rubber gloves.

Two years after the launch of its Marigold gloves the J. Allen Rubber Co. was taken over by United Transport. Sales boomed in the late 1950s, with production rising from 15,000 pairs in 1952 to 500,000 in 1959. Marigold gloves were exported all over the world, especially to the USA, where Playtex was its main competitor, and Europe, where Scandinavia and Italy were the main markets.

Rubber gloves are manufactured by dipping porcelain formers into liquid latex and then curing the resulting film. These surgeons' gloves are made so that they are uniformly .012 inches (0.3 mm) thick.

The London Rubber Co., which had its own Suregrip rubber gloves and was well known for its Durex condoms, bought the Marigold brand in 1960. With its production and marketing expertise the company developed the range still further. By the 1990s 35 million pairs of household rubber gloves were being sold each year in Britain alone.

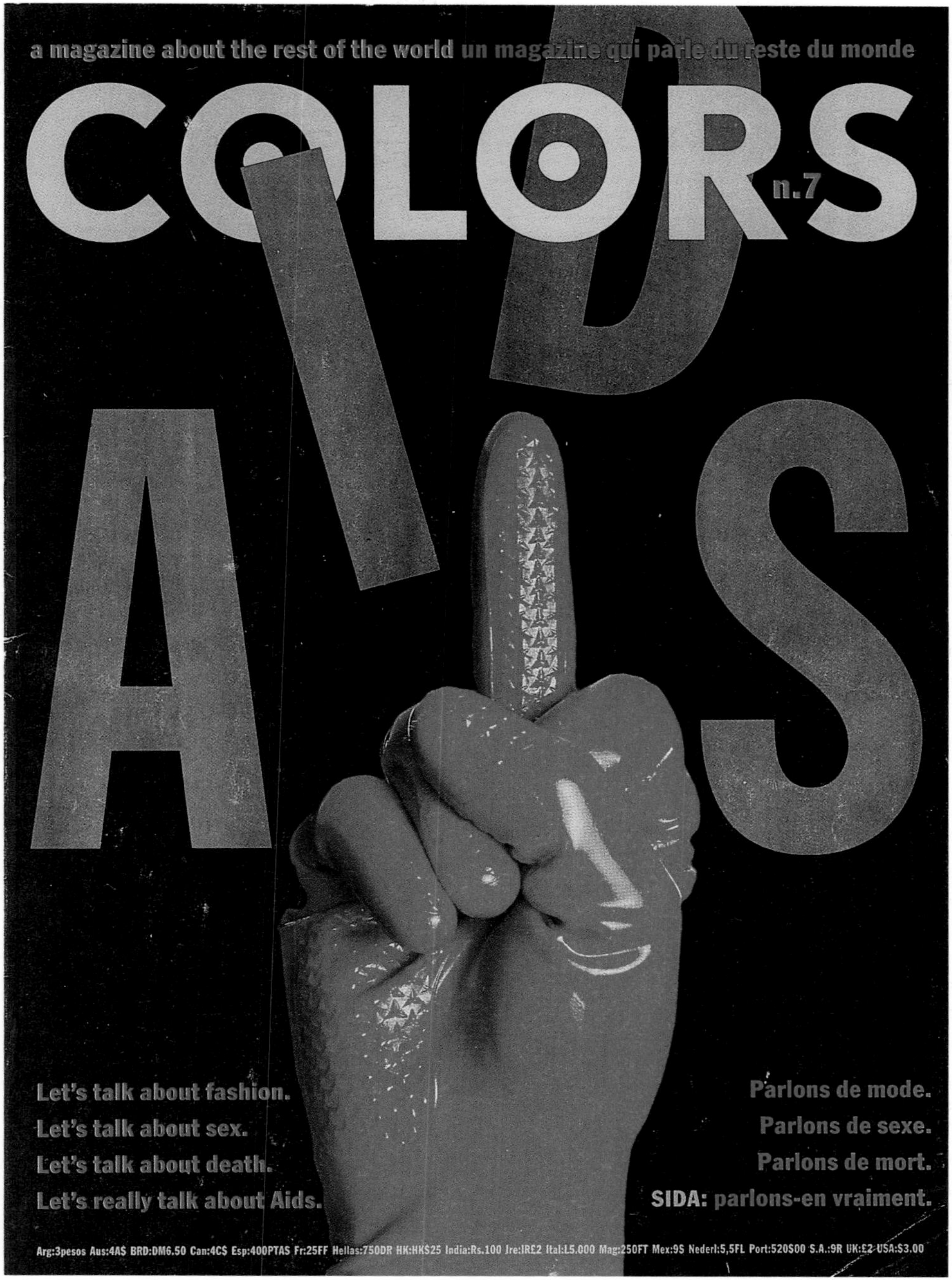

a magazine about the rest of the world un magazine qui parle du reste du monde
COLORS
n.7
AIDS
Let's talk about fashion.
Let's talk about sex.
Let's talk about death.
Let's really talk about Aids.
Parlons de mode.
Parlons de sexe.
Parlons de mort.
SIDA: parlons-en vraiment.
Arg:3pesos Aus:4A$ BRD:DM6.50 Can:4C$ Esp:400PTAS Fr:25FF Hellas:750DR HK:HK$25 India:Rs.100 Ire:IR£2 Ital:L5.000 Mag:250FT Mex:9$ Nederl:5,5FL Port:520$00 S.A.:9R UK:£2 USA:$3.00

Benetton is an Italian clothes manufacturer well known for its colourful jumpers. Its 'United Colors of Benetton' advertising campaign which started in the early 1990s did not try to sell clothes at all but attracted attention to the brand name by taking an uncosy view of 'real world' issues. Colors magazine is produced in support of the same cause, or causes, depending on how you look at it. The special AIDS issue was published in June 1994 with creative direction by Tibor Kalman.

Milk carton

In 1951 the Swedish industrialist Ruben Rausing created the tetrahedral carton that became a global phenomenon and made him a fortune. The Tetra Pak was launched in 1952 as a totally new kind of packaging in the way it worked, in the way it stacked easily and in its manufacture and low cost. Appearing first as a milk carton, by the 1990s it was commonly being used for a range of different liquid foodstuffs from soup to wine.

Ruben Rausing was a specialist in packaging for dry foodstuffs such as flour and sugar, and he used all his experience and the latest packaging technologies in developing the Tetra Pak. His aim was to combine paper, aluminium and plastic into a design that would ensure that milk always reached the consumer in hygienic condition, while also making distribution easier and more efficient.

The event that really saw the new packaging come into its own was in 1961, when the Tetra Pak became the first aseptically filled carton for UHT long-life milk. By the 1990s, Tetra Paks were being made under licence all around the world.

In the early 1980s milk cartons in America began to appear with the faces of missing children printed on one side with pleas for sightings by the public. The campaign has now been discontinued, but the idea was taken up by other organizations, including The Body Shop.

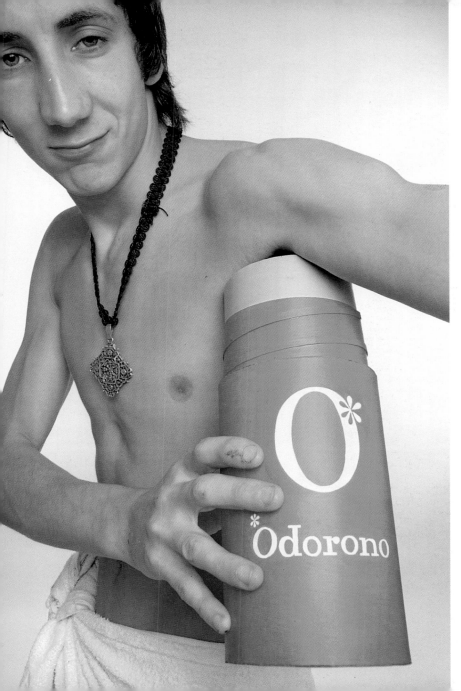

Roll-on deodorant

Looking for better ways of applying the new deodorants produced by Mum in the 1930s, a company product developer in Britain was contemplating one of the new ballpoint pens which had been introduced after the war and came up with the idea of using the same technique for applying deodorant. Regional test marketing of the first roll-ons was undertaken in the USA in 1952. Ban Roll-on was introduced there in 1955 and in Britain as Mum Rollette in 1958.

Masking – or complementing – body smells with perfumes is as old as civilization. But splashing on a little rosewater is no substitute for taking a bath, and the problem of preventing personal smells and sweat remained unsolved until this century.

Mum had in fact been responsible for the invention of a deodorant cream based on zinc oxide in Philadelphia as far back as 1888. It came in a round

Pete Townshend was lead guitarist of The Who, the band that had a number of hits in the 1960s starting with 'My Generation' and that also made a habit of smashing up their guitars and amps on stage. The cover shot for The Who Sell Out album, released in 1967, had an outsize roll-on deodorant made by Roger Law, who later made the satirical puppets for Spitting Image, with photograph by David Montgomery and design by David King.

tin and was applied with the fingers. But what was really needed was something that effectively deodorized at the same time as retarding sweat. In the 1900s anti-perspirants became available, based on a solution of aluminium chloride. They did work, although they tended to be wet and sticky and could also irritate the skin as well as damage clothes.

Alternative chemicals such as aluminium sulphate were used in the 1930s and by the end of the decade most of the effectiveness problems had been solved. An ingredient of some deodorants called zirconium did cause a scare in the 1970s when it was linked with cancer, and more recently the aluminium that is the base of most deodorant formulations has been linked with Alzheimer's disease, although there is no evidence that wearing deodorants predisposes anyone to the condition.

Deodorant 'delivery systems' began to be resolved into three main contenders: aerosol spray, solid stick and roll-on. Sprays often took too long to dry and didn't always go where they were meant to and aerosol cans ran into trouble in the 1970s when their CFC propellants were blamed for depleting the ozone layer in the atmosphere. Solid sticks have survived but have always taken second place to roll-ons, which had soon become the norm, proving themselves to be the most successful and effective way of delivering deodorant ingredients directly without mess or bother.

Fish Fingers/ Sticks

In America it remains the lowly fish stick, in Italy it is an expensive delicacy, but in Britain it has become perhaps the most popular convenience food ever. When Fish Fingers were introduced to the British nation by Birds Eye in 1955 an institution was created.

Despite the food rationing after the war, Britain always had plenty of fish. It was cheap and nutritious and a good source of protein for growing children. The government recommended it to the family, but children weren't that keen when it meant taking out bones and fiddling about with bits of skin on their plates. Neither did their mothers find preparing fish quite as convenient as they might wish.

It was the people at Birds Eye who turned their attention to producing fish in a form that was easily prepared, inexpensive and appealed to children. Birds Eye was the only frozen food brand in Britain in the early 1950s (see also Frozen food, page 71) and they had already introduced whole

Britain prizes its cod — and so does Iceland. In 1976 the Cod War flared up as a result of a dispute over fishing rights in the North Atlantic. The confrontation descended into farce when the Icelanders attacked the Royal Navy with carrots, although this ramming by a gunboat was more serious.

frozen fillets of fish to the market. In America a Birds Eye team discovered an obscure frozen product called Fish Sticks – boneless, oblong pieces of fish covered in breadcrumbs ready for grilling or frying, made by Gorton's. This was the answer.

Herring was the most plentiful fish around the British Isles at the time, so Birds Eye first produced what they called the Herring Savoury, a stick-shaped portion coated in batter and breadcrumbs. For comparative test-marketing purposes they also made the same item using cod. The research delivered the unequivocal verdict that it was the cod version and not the Herring Savoury that people preferred. The Herring Savoury was dropped and cod Fish Fingers were born.

In 1956 Birds Eye used the new commercial television channel to establish Fish Fingers with the family. The famous Captain Birds Eye character was introduced in 1967 in a series of TV commercials that has lasted over 30 years. The first ever radio commercial transmitted in Britain was also for Birds Eye Fish Fingers. The 60-second commercial went out from London Broadcasting on 8 October 1973 at 6.08 a.m.

Now Fish Fingers have become part of the British family way of life. Indeed, one of the complaints expatriate housewives had when interviewed in Kuwait after the invasion by Iraq that led to the Gulf War was that Fish Fingers for their children were no longer available in local supermarkets.

Disposable syringe

The problems associated with cleaning and sterilizing the old reusable type of hypodermic syringes were highlighted with the advent of penicillin after its discovery in 1928. The residues of penicillin and other antibiotics have a habit of crystallizing within the syringe when left for any length of time, making it very difficult to clean and sterilize. By the 1950s the development of plastic technology began to allow for the high-volume manufacture of disposable plastic syringes which were much more reliable and always sterile.

A single-use glass syringe was first produced by leading American manufacturer Becton Dickinson for the 1954 field trials of Dr Jonas Salk's vaccine for polio involving four million American schoolchildren. With their glass bodies and metal needle hubs these syringes were not cost effective, and disposing of them safely was also a difficulty. By the 1970s Becton Dickinson had completely converted to true disposable syringes with plastic bodies and needle hubs. In the early 1950s the company could produce around 150,000 reusable syringes a week. When transition to disposables was complete production capability had reached 14 million a week.

Disposable syringes are issued by travel agents for those going to risky parts of the world.

STERILE MED

KEEP PACK AWAY

CONTENTS

1 ---- Medical Card
6 ---- Cleansing Medi-Sw
6 ---- Pre-Injection Swab
3 ---- 21g x 1½" Hypode
3 ---- 25g x ⅝" Hypoder
3 ---- 2ml Hypodermic S
1 ---- Braided Silk Suture
1 ---- Adhesive Suture 1
2 ---- Airstrip Plasters

Distributed

CJL TRA
HEATHCOAT
20 SAVILE
LONDON W
TEL. 01-43
A.B.T.A. 1

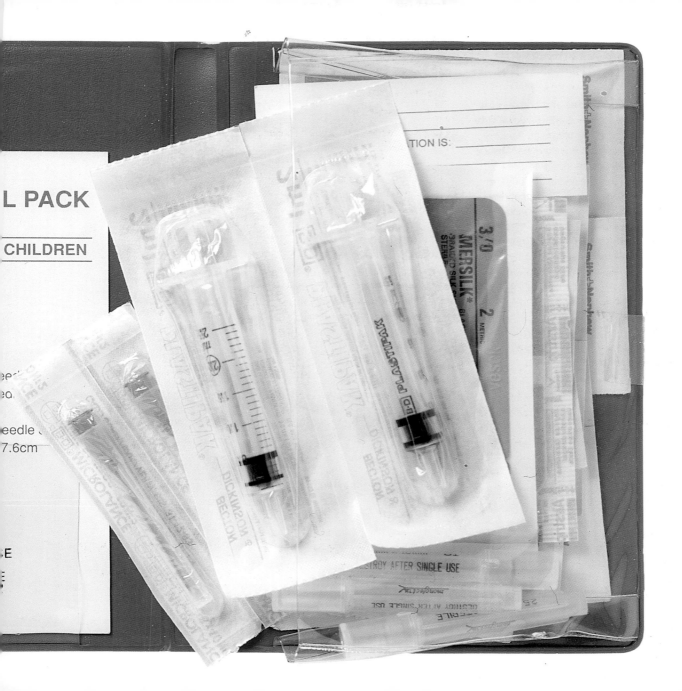

The Pill

It was the realization of a dream, especially for women – a pill you could take to stop you getting pregnant. As early as 1937, research chemists had discovered that hormones could be used to make oral contraceptives. In 1950, Dr Gregory Pincus began the pioneering research on behalf of the Planned Parenthood Movement in the USA that led to the first approved and commercially available pill in 1960.

The first type of Pill contained the hormones oestrogen and progestogen, which interfered with the normal processes of the menstrual cycle and suppressed ovulation. It was, however, more than the technical breakthrough that made the Pill so important. It also represented and fuelled the changing attitudes to sex and birth control, known as the 'sexual revolution', which preoccupied a number of Western societies in the late 1950s and early 1960s. The huge emotional and social implications stemmed from the new and different kinds of freedoms it gave to partners – freedom from responsibility for the man and freedom to take responsibility for the woman. Both partners also loved it because it allowed for completely natural sex,

The Health Education Council ran a famous poster campaign in 1971 for the Family Planning Association promoting contraception. The photo was by Alan Brooking.

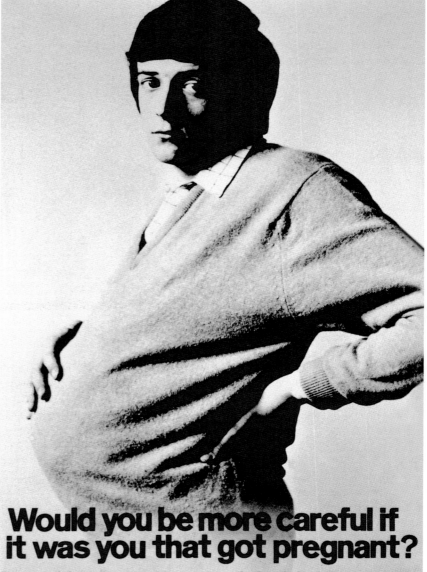

Would you be more careful if it was you that got pregnant?

Anyone married or single can get advice on contraception from the Family Planning Association. Margaret Pyke House, 27-35 Mortimer Street, London W1 N 8BQ. Tel. 01-636 9135.

The Health Education Council

without distraction from any contraptions, while being simple and almost foolproof provided it was taken properly.

The first large-scale trials of the Pill were conducted by Dr Pincus and began in 1956 with over 1,000 volunteers from San Juan, Puerto Rico. Over a period of three years, only 17 of the women became pregnant. The Pill became commercially available in 1960 as a product called Enovid 10, marketed by the Illinois-based G. D. Searle Drug Co. The same year, Searle conducted the first field tests in Britain and the Pill went on sale there in 1961.

Resisted by various religious and spiritual organizations, notably the Roman Catholic Church, it was predominantly the Protestant countries of the West that first took to the Pill. By 1965 it had overtaken the condom as the most popular contraceptive in Britain and looked set to consign other contraceptive devices to history. Over the years the composition of the Pill changed markedly, with the dose of steroid reduced and some progestogens abandoned.

Then in 1969 cardiovascular problems associated with the levels of oestrogen in the Pill came to light. These health scares were followed by the growth of AIDS, and 'safe sex' took on a new meaning in the 1980s and 1990s. The Pill's popularity declined and barrier methods made a comeback – not only to prevent conception, which was the point of the Pill, but almost more importantly to prevent disease.

As part of their Eurovision Song Contest act in 1981, Britain's Bucks Fizz girls ripped off their Velcro-secured skirts, and won the competition.

Velcro

The invention of Velcro was inspired by the way burs attached themselves to clothes. The particular clothes in question belonged to Swiss inventor George de Mestral, who realized that nature's technique could be used to make fasteners. It took him 15 years to develop his idea and he patented Velcro in 1956, starting production the following year. He took the name for his new product from *velours*, velvet, and *crochet*, hook.

It was in 1941, when de Mestral was hunting in the woods of the Jura region just across the Swiss border in France, that he started to wonder how it was that burs attached themselves to his clothes and the coat of his dog. He later examined a bur under his microscope and found that its bristly hairs were in fact tiny hooks that fastened themselves to equally tiny loops and hairs in fabric and fur. His first idea was to use the discovery to make a new type of clothes fastener.

It took de Mestral eight years to solve the problems of attaching the minuscule hooks and loops to a tape backing. Then he had to find ways of mechanizing the production which involved weaving the Velcro with 300 nylon hooks and loops per square inch. He formed an association with

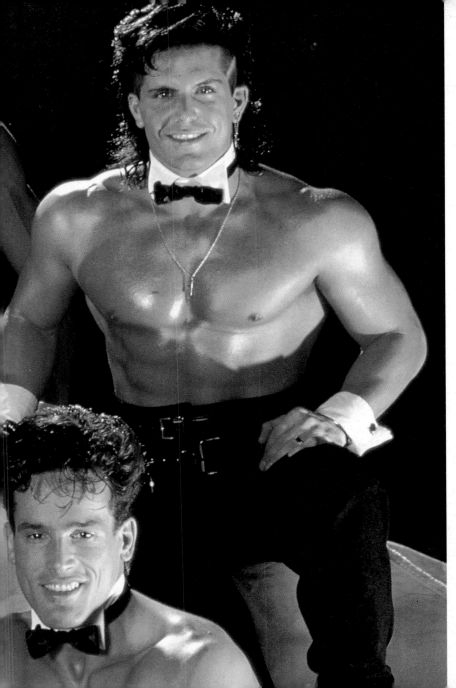

Jakob Müller, manufacturers of narrow fabric looms, and in 1957 finally set up production in Aubonne.

De Mestral later sold his company and worldwide rights to a Swiss company, Velcro SA, and Velok Ltd of Montreal bought the rights to make Velcro throughout North and South America, Australasia and parts of Asia. This part of the enterprise expanded, changed its name to Velcro Industries Ltd and became the largest member of the Velcro empire, whose headquarters are in the Netherlands.

It was not the clothing industry that originally took to Velcro. Instead its first real success came in the early 1960s when aerospace companies started using it for attaching insulation to the insides of aircraft. Soon it was used in all jet aircraft built in the USA, and then in spacecraft – ending up on the moon in the spacesuits of Neil Armstrong and Buzz Aldrin in 1969. Consumer industries finally took to Velcro in the 1970s, and it became common as a fastening for shoes, wallets, jackets, bras and children's clothes.

Velcro allows the apparently effortless disrobing of The Chippendales, as they throw off their sailor suits in part of their male stripper act. Described as 'America's Hottest Export', the group of 16 lovely boys started touring the world in 1991. Considering they can only appeal to half the population, the fact that The Chippendales have sold two million tickets in Britain alone is testimony to the pulling power of the lads and the sense of humour of women.

143

Disposable nappies/ diapers

Procter and Gamble tested its first design for disposable diapers in Dallas, Texas, during the summer of 1956. Nobody much liked them, especially when the weather was hot. The company tried again with a number of improvements in March 1959, choosing Rochester, New York this time. The trials were encouraging, if not overwhelmingly conclusive, and the company began to develop its mass production processes. It named the new product Pampers.

Procter and Gamble became interested in the first place when its director of exploratory development, Vic Mills, was given the task of looking after his newborn grandchild and did not take too well to changing and cleaning towelling diapers, or terry nappies as they are called in Britain. He came to the conclusion that there must be a better way of dealing with what babies do. So he put his researchers to work on the development of an effective disposable diaper.

It was hard for the new disposables to change the habits of generations, and early sales were not quick to build. Further test marketing was carried out in Peoria, Illinois in December 1961, which revealed price problems with the new product. But when the production process had been developed to allow more competitive pricing, the disposable diaper did begin to win acceptance.

The prototypes used in the early tests consisted of tape-on and pin-on versions of a basic absorbent cellulose pad inside plastic pants. Before Pampers there had been some pricey paper diapers around, including Drypers in the USA and Paddipads in Britain. But these were not particularly babyproof, and tended to be used only in emergencies. In 1956 they accounted for just one per cent of the market. Today well over 90 per cent of nappy changes are made with disposables — practically 100 per cent in France.

Since the early days a number of advances have made parents and babies even happier. These include leg elastic, stronger linings, the replacement of cellulose wadding with superabsorbent granular materials, a wider range of different sizes and special designs for boys and girls. The only problem that now remains is how best to dispose of the disposable so that it doesn't affect the environment, let alone block up the drains.

The 'throw-away society' has a price. Consumer convenience and good business are not always compatible with the wider environmental effect and cost. Making people aware of the issues since the 1970s has been the job of green lobby groups such as Friends of the Earth and Greenpeace while companies such as The Body Shop have showed that there needn't be a conflict.

250 trees a year are used to

10 00 tons of disposable nappi

5 00 tons of untreated body e

6 00 nappy changes are made

250 hours are spent in nappi

facture disposables nappies

tossed in landfills each day

ent is brought to landfills via disposable nappies

ig the baby's first years of life

babies

Superglue

The glue that needs no time or air to dry was invented by Dr Vernon Krieble of Hartford, Connecticut. He called it Loctite. Working in the laboratories of Trinity College he developed the cure inhibition system for a liquid bonding resin that hardened in the absence of air. The name was coined by his wife Nancy and the new 'superglue' was announced at the University Club, New York, on 26 July 1956. By 1975 sales had reached $67 million. Eastman Kodak had also come up with a bonding agent while searching for materials with the same refractive index as glass to be used in the company's photographic equipment. The substance stuck glass together rock solidly and as a result an adhesive was marketed in the 1950s, but only for specialist industrial use.

Commercial superglue's only problem was that it was too good and mishaps occurred with people ending up in hospital with bits of their bodies stuck together. This gave the press some good copy but only caused a hiccup in the progress of superglues. They came to Britain in 1976 and were soon available throughout the world.

Overleaf: Introduced in 1950, Araldite is a credible rival to the superglues, although it requires the mixing of a resin and hardener before use. Like the superglues it forms an immensely strong bond and has retained a fair share of the market through the 1990s.

Cling film/ Cling wrap

Thin sheets of PVC (polyvinylchloride) on a roll were introduced commercially in the USA in 1958. Used for wrapping, the material stretches and shrinks back to a close fit, clinging to itself and making an air-tight seal. It is also strong and transparent. These properties make it ideal for food in the fridge or lunchbox, keeping moisture in and bacteria out. Known as cling wrap or food wrap in America and cling film in Britain, it has become an indispensable kitchen item.

The use of plastics for wrapping started when Swiss chemist Dr Jacques Brandenberger, working in Zurich, used regenerated cellulose to make a thin, flexible sheet in 1908. He called it Cellophane and it began to be made in Paris in 1912. In America after the First World War Du Pont improved the water-resistance of Cellophane, widening its usefulness. As the century progressed advances in technology brought prices down and introduced the new plastics, of which PVC has become one of the most important

Mostly derived from petroleum, plastics are cheap and have become the prime material of the throw-away

Wrapping up in plastic film is meant to be an aid to losing weight. From The Full Monty, *a low-budget British film which was a hit in 1997 receiving Oscar nominations in 1998.*

society. Towards the end of the century the huge amounts being dumped have raised increasing concern for their effect on the environment. So biodegradable plastics have begun to be introduced as alternatives. Of these PHB (polyhydroxybutyrate) is made from sugar and is digested by soil micro-organisms; Biopol, developed in 1990, is actually produced by micro-organisms and breaks down into carbon dioxide and water in landfill sites.

Pizza delivery

Second only to the hamburger as the world's favourite fast food, the pizza has the unique distinction of usually being eaten at home, although prepared and cooked at the local pizzeria. With companies falling over themselves to promise ever-shorter delivery times, a telephone call will bring the pizza you desire to your door in a few minutes.

Pizza deliveries almost certainly started in the late 1950s in New York, home of the Italian immigrant and also the place where the first pizzeria opened in 1905. Pizza had already become a favourite takeaway, remaining hot and not becoming too soggy on the journey home. So, in a city where businesses have a tradition of delivering almost anything the customer wants, enterprising pizzerias began to include home delivery. Many pizza companies now do nothing else. The world's largest pizza delivery company is Domino's, which has 6,000 outlets in 60 countries and in 1996 had record sales of $2.8 billion.

The modern pizza – and the first pizza delivery – are attributed to a baker called Raphael Esposito, in Naples, who created a special version of what was then a simple peasant dish for the visit of King Umberto and Queen Margherita in 1889. Called pizza margherita to this day, it consisted of red tomatoes, white mozzarella and green basil, which are the colours of the Italian flag.

Pizza migrated to the USA with the Italians, but it was after the Second World War, when returning GIs created a nationwide demand for the food they had loved so much in Italy, that it became such big business. American pizzas are now a far cry from their Italian ancestors. All sorts of different crusts – thin, deep-dish, stuffed – are loaded with toppings of every imaginable complexion and derivation, including Indian, Mexican and Chinese.

Car seat belt

The first car to be equipped with a three-point adjustable safety belt as a standard feature was the Volvo PV544 in 1959. Patented by one of its engineers, Nils Bohlin, Volvo showed remarkable magnanimity in deliberately not enforcing its rights to the device, in the belief that all motorists should benefit from the obvious advantages of the belt. Thus other manufacturers have been able to produce them easily and without licence, to the benefit of drivers and passengers.

It took a long time to overcome considerable resistance from the motoring public to the wearing of seat belts. There was a feeling that being told what to do in the privacy of one's car infringed personal rights and freedoms. Most countries tried to persuade people to wear their seat belts voluntarily before enforcing it by law. This led to campaigns on TV and in the press using such slogans as 'buckle up' in the USA and 'clunk click with every trip' in Britain (the 'clunk' being the door and the 'click' being the belt).

In 1969 Czechoslovakia became the first country to make the wearing of

Showing crash testing of seat belts with dummies became part of Volvo's advertising strategy as it claimed the high ground in car safety. The company also introduced the inertia reel in 1968, allowing the belt to take up slack as well as to retract when not in use, while locking it in a crash.

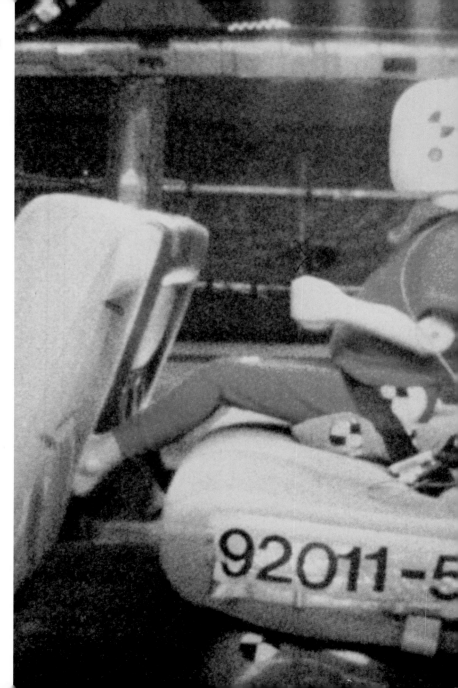

seat belts compulsory. Britain's law came into force in 1983. In the USA it has been left to the individual states, and towards the end of the 1990s only New Hampshire still does not require adults to wear seat belts. Despite this, only 68 per cent of adults actually buckle up in the USA, compared with around 80 per cent in Britain and 90 per cent elsewhere in Europe. In the ten years up to 1996 it is reckoned that seat belts prevented 55,600 deaths and 1.3 million injuries on America's roads.

Lycra

The elastane fibre called Lycra was introduced by Du Pont in 1959, the latest in a line of polymer 'wonder fibres' that started in 1938 with nylon. It is so elastic that it can be stretched between four and seven times its length and, when relaxed, will instantly recover its original length and tension, time after time. It also has between two and three times the restraining power of rubber, and one-third the weight.

Lycra made its first commercial appearance in 1960 when underwear manufacturers started to use it – Warner Bros for its step-in girdles and a year later Berlei for its bras. The fashionability of the new material became assured in 1965 when a report on swimwear made with Lycra appeared in *Vogue*, saying: 'When it's dried in the sun, it's a sinuous velvety black, and when it's soaked with water it glistens like

a seal on the rocks.'

Lycra is now commonly found combined with other fibres, such as cotton and nylon, in all sorts of garments – swimsuits, hosiery and lingerie – and has even been used for the tent-like roofs of modern buildings.

But Lycra's particular popularity is in sports clothes, and there are some suggestions that it actually improves the performance of professional sporting figures, especially athletes at the top level. Where the slightest advantage can make a difference in competitive results, athletes may benefit from Lycra's high stretch and compression qualities, reducing muscle vibration and thus muscle fatigue. Acting as a second skin, it may also enhance the feedback of muscle performance information to the brain. Whatever the truth in this, being taut and glossy, showing every body contour, every muscle ripple, Lycra certainly makes athletes look good.

Overleaf: Linford Christie, Britain's greatest ever sprint athlete, became famous for his Lycra gear, although it's not clear whether it made him run any faster. He was European 200-metre champion in 1986 and 100-metre champion in 1990. He was Commonwealth 100-metre champion in 1986 and again in 1990. He was Olympic 100-metre champion in 1992 and World 100-metre champion in 1993. In addition, he was European indoor 200-metre champion in 1986 and 60-metre champion in 1990. He also became captain of the British Men's Athletics Team, a commentator and a much-respected sporting ambassador.

Plastic garbage bag

Before plastic refuse sacks, rubbish was tipped directly into bins and then collected by the local authority. This meant smell and bits of rubbish all over the road in the wake of dust carts. It was the local authorities that first supplied plastic bags for containing rubbish to make it easier to collect, more hygienic and certainly less odorous.

ICI's invention of polythene in 1933 led to the first instance of polythene film being made in 1937. In 1954 a bubble-blowing process was used to begin commercial production of film at Hillhouse near Blackpool. In the late 1950s polythene film also became an important product for supermarkets, which used it extensively for wrapping.

ICI then diversified from simply selling sheets of polythene film to making products from it. Among these were carrier bags for shops and Britain's first 'black bag' refuse sacks, which were introduced and adopted by Hitchin Council in Hertfordshire in 1960. In 1963 an ICI subsidiary, British Visqueen Ltd, was formed to concentrate on film products, and now produces billions of sacks a year.

Plastic bags came to the rescue of the Prince Charles, Princess Diana and John Major when the heavens opened at Luciano Pavarotti's concert in London's Hyde Park on 30 July 1991.

Ring-pull/ pull-top

Despite its novelty, the first beer to be sold in cans in the 1950s did not sell too well because it required a separate can opener to get at the contents. In 1962 Alcoa showed the Iron City Brewery Company of Pittsburg a new type of can that had a ring attached to the top. When you pulled the ring back it tore open a pre-scored keyhole aperture. No more can openers; the container had become self-contained. In October that year, the Iron City Brewery became the first beverage manufacturer to sell the new pull-top, or ring-pull as it became known in Britain. Tear-off closures had already been introduced with varying degrees of success for bottle tops, easy-open sardine tins, even hot-dog sausage tins. But the beer can with aluminium pull-top was turned down by a number of the big American brewing companies before Schlitz took it on. Then the others quickly followed suit. During 1964 sales of beer in cans jumped by 1.5 billion units, of which 70 per cent in

Ring-pull crime broke out in the 1960s when it was realised that the rings fitted parking meters and jammed them. In those days a broken meter meant that you could park there free. Changes in the parking rules and the design of the meters, as well as the demise of the ring-pull in favour of the snap-top, soon put a stop to the problem.

cans had the now-familiar keyhole top.

For most of the century cans had been made of tin plate. Even with the new pull-tops aluminium was still only used for drinks at the top end of the market. In 1962 Alcoa and Anheuser-Busch, the brewers of Budweiser, formed a subsidiary company to manufacture all-aluminium cans. Improved production meant more competitive costs. Beer brewers as well as soft-drinks manufacturers soon began to convert to all-aluminium containers. By 1997 worldwide annual sales of aluminium canned beverages topped 160 billion.

The original pull-tops had one disadvantage. The ring with the attached piece of the top had to be disposed of separately. So the next development was the snap-top can, where the opening mechanism stayed attached to the top after being bent back.

Silicone implant

The first silicone breast implant was carried out in the USA in 1962, using silicone gel produced by Dow Corning. For a while the technique was welcomed as a wonderful addition to cosmetic surgery. Then came a raft of lawsuits concerning claims that silicone implants cause a variety of health problems. The surgical technique has since become the subject of a number of rulings in America and Europe.

Silicone is an organic polymer containing silicon. Dow Corning and General Electric both had patents on silicone bouncing putty which their respective researchers had come across accidentally while working with silicon. Earl Warrick and R. R. McGregor received their patent in 1947 and it was assigned to Dow Corning. James Wright, a senior General Electric man who had been trying to make a hard synthetic rubber using silicon, received his patent in 1951. Apart from making bouncing toys, the discoveries proved to be of little use, but the projects did lead to the silicone gel used today in plastic surgery.

Silicon of course went on to find its true calling in silicon chips, the building blocks of information technology.

Pouches filled with silicone gel give women the shape and size of breasts they want.

Overleaf: Beloved Baywatch babe Pamela Anderson changed her breasts to make sure that she stood out in her role as CJ, some sort of Californian lifesaver, which she landed in 1992. As she said: 'I had implants, but so has every single person in Los Angeles'. Before she decided to change her shape, her bit parts had included TV appearances on the two comedy series Married ... with Children and Home Improvement. Frequent exposure in Playboy, including covers and the coveted centrefold; a stormy marriage with Tommy Lee, drummer of the group Motley Crue; and her hopeless 1996 movie Barb Wire, which flopped critically and at the box office, ensured that she became and remained a 1990s tabloid favourite.

interc

Sexual

ourse

began
In nineteen sixty-three
(Which was rather late for me) –
Between the end of the *Chatterly* ban
And the Beatles' first LP

Philip Larkin

Hover mower

Swedish inventor Karl Dahlman became fascinated by the idea of a lawn mower that needed no wheels, floating on a cushion of air instead. He spent a long time researching and developing the technology required and in 1963 finally came up with his first hover-mower model, which he called the Flymo – the flying mower. The Flymo company became part of Electrolux in 1969, based in Britain, and has since become Europe's largest manufacturer of powered lawn mowers, accounting for almost half of the market in Britain and selling in 50 countries around the world.

The Flymo was inspired by the hovercraft developed by Christopher Cockerell, an electronics engineer and part-time boat builder, which he patented on 12 December 1955. He had begun his experiments using two different sized tin cans, one inside the other, attached to a nozzle blowing air from a vacuum cleaner. He found that the downward pressure exerted by his device was three times that of the air coming out of the nozzle by itself. This eventually led to the launch of the $3\frac{1}{2}$ ton SR-N1 hovercraft on 30 May 1959 at Cowes in the Isle of Wight.

The Flymo lawn mower had become well known by the time its giant cousin, the world's largest hovercraft, was launched in 1978. Named the Princess Anne, it was operated by British Rail Seaspeed across the Channel.

Using the same principle, the Flymo has a fan and skirt and makes mowing very easy, especially over hilly slopes, by floating just above the grass. It took a while to overcome the natural resistance of users, but soon they realized that the Flymo was more than a gimmick. People started to believe the slogan 'It's much less bovver with a hover' in the lawn-mower wars which were fought out by competing brands, a feature of advertising in the springtime during the 1970s and 1980s.

Moog synthesizer

Budding physicist Robert Moog met composer Herbert Deutsch at a conference in 1963 and discovered that they shared an enthusiasm for electronic music. They collaborated in trying out the effect of a number of new electronic circuits, and in August 1964 Moog built the prototype of his synthesizer, which he described as 'voltage-controlled electronic music modules'. This allowed the performer to create sounds by connecting modules with electric wires and turning knobs.

An electronic machine that synthesized musical notes had been made by RCA in 1955. It was operated by punched tape and was enormous and unwieldy, taking up half a room. Like its more sophisticated successor, the RCA Mark 2, which came out in 1959, it was mainly a scientific experiment, and

few musicians got near it.

Moog was studying for his doctorate in physics at Cornell University and first exhibited his electronic music maker at the Audio Engineering Society Convention of 1964 in New York. From the age of 14 he had been building theremins, strange instruments which had been around since their invention in 1920 by the Russian, Leon Theremin. They produced low-frequency oscillations audible to the human ear by mixing high-frequency oscillations from vacuum tubes.

Following favourable reactions to his first synthesizer, Moog made four large modular versions intended to be used as installations in recording studios. After a concert with one of these at the Museum of Modern Art in New York he put them all up for sale to raise money for development. Keith Emerson of the group Emerson, Lake and Palmer bought the first through a distributor in London.

Popular music got wind of the Moog synthesizer and the Beach Boys used it in 'Good Vibrations', which became a number one hit in 1966. In 1967 the Beatles bought one, as did Mick Jagger for the Rolling Stones. In 1971 the MiniMoog was launched, completely portable and well liked by rock bands. By the end of the century keyboard-operated electronic synthesized sounds were almost as essential as the ubiquitous electric guitar across all kinds of factional dance and mainstream pop as well as in jazz and film music.

Mick Jagger bought one of the first the Moog synthesizers for the Rolling Stones in 1967. Called the greatest rock 'n' roll band in the world, they are certainly the most enduring. Jagger, Brian Jones, Keith Richards, Bill Wyman and Charlie Watts formed the group in 1961 and in 1998 all but two of the original line-up (Jones died of an overdose in 1969 and Wyman has retired) embarked on their umpteenth concert world tour. The first Rolling Stones single in 1963 was a version of Chuck Berry's 'Come On'. Other definitive hits include 'The Last Time' in 1965 and 'Jumpin' Jack Flash' and 'Honky Tonk Women' in 1968.

Right: *Switched-on Bach by Walter Carlos in 1968 was a recording of Bach's music performed on a Moog synthesizer. The popularity of the album confirmed the legitimacy of Moog's machine as a serious musical instrument.*

Miniskirt

It was the collection of André Courrèges shown in Paris in 1964 that started it. He did away with the innocent, unfitted, little-girl dresses of the early 1960s and presented innovative, space-age clean lines, materials and colours – and short skirts worn with boots. In December 1965 miniskirts a good six inches (15 cm) above the knee were seen in the King's Road, Chelsea.

In 1965 leading British model Jean Shrimpton caused a flutter when she appeared to present the fashion prize to the best-dressed woman attending the Melbourne Cup, one of Australia's premier horse races. Unlike all those around her she was hatless, wore no gloves or stockings – and her hemline was daringly high.

Although inspired by Courrèges in Paris, the miniskirt became a phenomenon of 'swinging' London, championed by British designers such as Mary Quant. The mini even helped to change the way clothes were sold. Determinedly expressing their new freedom, young women preferred to buy their minis from the 'hip' independent boutiques of the King's Road and Carnaby Street rather than the traditional large department stores.

The mini was a symbol of revolution. It even caused a tax problem. Children's clothes were sold tax-free in Britain, the authorities having regulations that determined whether a dress was a woman's or a child's by the length of the skirt. With the advent of such short skirts that distinction disappeared and new rules had to be drawn up in 1965 taking account of bust size as well.

The fashion scene, which had been a slave to the big couture houses, was freed in the 1960s and gave way to a more eclectic approach for the rest of the century. Miniskirts became just one more element of the designers' repertoire and an accepted part of any woman's wardrobe. In the 1990s the French designer Jean-Paul Gaultier even tried to introduce miniskirts for men, but he seemed to be the only person prepared to wear them.

Miniskirts remained fashionable in the 1990s – here worn by supermodels Claudia Schiffer (Chanel), Naomi Campbell (Galliano) and Stephanie Seymour (Chanel).

Maclaren baby buggy/carriage

The children's push-chair took a giant leap forward when former test pilot and retired aeronautical engineer Owen Finlay Maclaren took out a patent for a new type of buggy in July 1965. By the end of 1967 he had made just over a thousand Maclaren buggies. By the 1990s production had reached half a million a year.

Owen Maclaren brought his considerable knowledge of lightweight load-bearing structures, accumulated during his aeronautical engineering career, to the problem of redesigning the push-chair. The beauty of the new design was its lightness — with its aluminium frame it weighed just 6 lb (3 kg) — and its three-dimensional folding mechanism that collapsed the buggy like an umbrella. As a design director at his company later said, 'he solved a very difficult three-dimensional fold problem. Today we are using computer-aided design systems to model solutions like that.'

Maclaren set up production of his original 'baby buggy' in his own converted stables. By 1976 output reached almost 600,000, of which 280,000 were exported. The company then began to expand the product range and a pram buggy was introduced which was a folding pram, carrycot and buggy all in one. Working with ICI, Maclaren also developed that year the processing and production required to make the new resilient balloon-foam tyres which further cushioned the ride of the already-comfortable buggies.

Owen Maclaren died in 1978 but the company had by then assumed his enterprising spirit and continued to expand and diversify. In 1983 the E-Type was introduced, which became the biggest selling Maclaren buggy, and the following year the Maclaren Sovereign started to make major inroads into important exports markets such as the USA. Maclaren Ltd today is a highly successful business consistently winning design and safety awards for a wide range of products, all variations on the original theme.

The Maclaren buggy's wheels and folding mechanism reflect the inventor's special knowledge and experience of aeronautical engineering.

Workmate

The extraordinary workbench-cum-vice-cum-sawhorse that has become an essential part of any self-respecting home-improvement enthusiast's equipment was originally designed by Ron Hickman, a project engineer at Lotus Cars, who patented his Minibench in 1968. He had been to see Black and Decker with an earlier design the year before, but was turned down. Late in 1968 he started to produce the units himself. After a change of heart, Black and Decker took on the idea and began making the Workmate in 1972. In 1975 it was launched in the USA and by the 1990s 20 million Workmates had been sold around the world.

Ron Hickman had spent nine years with Lotus. He was principal designer on the Elan Plus 2 and Europa models, and among his many innovations was the Lotus's pop-up headlamps, since copied around the world.

He left Lotus to concentrate on a number of ideas for new products. He had already started to develop his new workbench, which was prompted by an incident that occurred while sawing some wood in his house: he had been using a rather nice Windsor chair as a bench and wasn't too pleased when he realized he had sawn the chair as well as the piece of wood. Originally designed for his own use, the more he developed the workbench the more he was convinced he had created something that every do-it-yourself person would want.

The idea is based on two beams, one of which moves like a vice, that act as jaws to secure and clamp a wide range of different shapes, from planks of wood to drainpipes. Very lightweight and flexible, it can handle remarkably large jobs while remaining absolutely stable and, when not being used, it folds up to suitcase size.

Hickman went to see every manufacturer he could think of to get backing and, disappointed time and again,

finally set up his own company Mate-Tool, starting production in an old brewery. Sales climbed to 1,500 units in the first year and doubled in each of the next four years.

When Black and Decker came back to him, Hickman secured a deal with a new design, the Mark II Workmate, and handed it over to the company, who launched the product in 1972. There has been increasing success for the Workmate ever since.

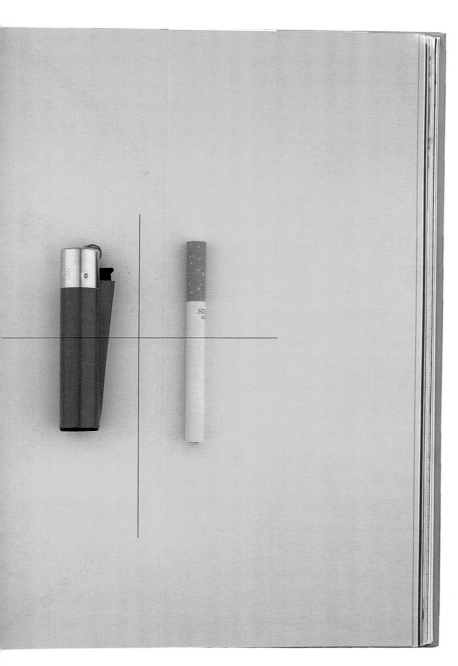

Disposable lighter

The French company Dupont, makers of highly desirable luxury cigarette lighters, had also developed the Cricket disposable lighter by the time it was taken over by Gillette in 1970. Under Gillette's wing the Cricket was marketed vigorously, and in 1972 it was introduced into the USA. Hot on its heels was a disposable lighter by Bic, the company that had popularized the throw-away ballpoint pen (see page 99). The two scrapped furiously for market ascendancy until 1984, when Gillette acknowledged defeat and sold Cricket to Swedish Match.

Smoking had been through its golden age by the time the cheap butane disposable lighters arrived. From the late 1920s to the 1960s it was solidly established as chic and fashionable social behaviour. All the trappings,

'Cigarettes are perfect, until you light them,' an insert for Parkett magazine in 1992 by Damien Hirst. The amount of attention that Hirst's work attracts has much to do with his talent for self-publicity. Forever known as the man who dunks dead animals in formaldehyde and displays them in glass tanks, he won the Turner Prize in 1995 and at the shortlist show erected Mother and Child Divided, four tanks containing the severed heads of cow and calf. Letters to The Times suggested that the Tate must be suffering from mad cow disease to allow it.

including expensive cigarette packaging, *objets d'art* ashtrays, silk smoking jackets, gold cigarette lighters, silver cigarette boxes and cases (Turkish on the left, Virginia on the right) supported the image. Smoking appealed equally to men and women. On the silver screen, alluring sirens posed languidly amid sublime curls of smoke while tall, quiet heroes with cigarillos stuck in the corners of their mouths dispatched the bad guys with intelligent ease.

As evidence mounted that smoking was directly implicated in the rise of lung and other cancers, as well as heart disease, the tide of opinion gradually turned against it. Doubts about smoking as a fashionable pastime arose as movie stars who had helped build the image died of smoking-related diseases. When people who had taken up smoking because its was cool tried to give up the habit, they discovered the true power of nicotine addiction. Growing antipathy towards the practice caused smokers to become as furtive as they had first been when they began to smoke at school

In many Western countries, governments, municipalities and transport authorities have banned smoking in public places. Restaurants have banned it also, although laws demanding no-smoking areas in French cafés and bars continue to be largely ignored. Offices banned it, so the sight of workers puffing outside the front entrance during breaks has become a common one. By the late 1990s, smoking in

California had been practically driven under ground.

All this proved to be a boon for the disposable lighter. Spending money on classy lighters is not the thing to do any more, and the disposable lighter has taken over – even to the point that when you try and buy a box of matches in the pub or bar you may well be offered a less expensive disposable lighter instead.

Child-resistant cap

The rise of consumerism in the USA during the 1960s led by such figures as Ralph Nader caused many manufacturers to look again at the safety of their products. One area of concern was the ease with which children could open their parents' pill containers.

In 1971, Owens-Brockway, a glass container manufacturer in the USA, introduced its first design to prevent children opening pill bottles. It was called the Clik-Lok and you had to push down on the cap quite hard and then turn it in order to get inside. Other designs were also introduced by rival manufacturers but the Clik-Lok became the standard and has been licensed to plastics manufacturers the world over. Now anything that can be deemed to be dangerous to children, from aspirin to paint remover, comes with a child-resistant cap.

On the image: PUSH DOWN AND UNSCREW

Pocket calculator

In 1972 Clive Sinclair in Britain produced the Sinclair Executive, a calculator that was truly pocket sized – a sleek, trim machine only ³/₈ inch (9.5 mm) thick and 5¹/₂ inches (140 mm) long. Its design set the standard. It had a light-emitting diode (LED) read-out display, a 7,000-transistor integrated circuit and was also the first calculator to be powered by a wafer-thin battery. As an essential item in modern life, the pocket calculator has become second only to the wristwatch. It has been responsible for a real revolution in day-to-day life, replacing jotted-down calculations and the need for anything but the most basic mental arithmetic.

A hand-held electronic calculator called the Pocketronic was introduced by Canon Business Machines in Tokyo on 15 April 1970. As it was not that small and had a rather cumbersome thermal-paper printout, its claim to be a pocket calculator was a little presumptuous. Texas Instruments, who had produced the first hand-held calculator in 1967, applied for a patent for its pocket calculator in 1972. In 1973 Hewlett Packard introduced pocket calculators tailored to particular needs, such as finance or economics, and in 1976 the company also began marketing programmable calculators, which were in effect pocket computers.

Starting off as expensive items, the

price soon came down, and pocket calculators began to be produced in their millions, in all shapes and sizes. Although the marvels of miniaturization are now taken for granted, making things smaller and smaller was still one of the main preoccupations of electronics research in the 1970s and early 1980s. By the 1990s calculators were typically powered by cells charged by light with memory storage and a wide range of mathematical functions.

Clive Sinclair, brilliant inventor of the pocket calculator in 1972, did not always cover himself in glory. The Sinclair C5 electric personal transport introduced with great fanfares in 1985 proved to be slow, fragile and vulnerable. Production was halted within two months.

LCD

The liquid crystal display (LCD) was patented by the chemical and pharmaceutical company Hoffman La Roche of Basle, Switzerland, in 1970. In the following years it made its appearance in the little windows that show the numbers on pocket calculators and digital watches. Because LCDs are flat they have become the most favoured method of display for an electronics industry always trying to save space. More recently they have also become familiar on mobile phones, laptop computers and mini-televisions.

A liquid crystal display consists of a substance with crystalline properties in a semi-liquid state sandwiched between polarizing filters similar to Polaroid sunglasses. When the display is blank the clusters of liquid crystal molecules are aligned in parallel formation. When an electric field is applied the molecules twist so that they reflect or transmit the polarized light falling on them.

Early LCDs could only display

LCDs tell passengers the speed and height of Concorde as it dashes across the Atlantic. After 14 years of development the Anglo-French plane became the world's first and, apart from a doomed Russian copy, the only supersonic airliner so far to operate scheduled commercial services. These were begun on 21 January 1976 when British Airways made its inaugural flight to New York and Air France did the same to Rio de Janeiro.

numbers, but with the development of dot matrix systems they also became capable of showing characters and graphics. The technology has since evolved from monochrome to colour, from still images to moving images and finally from small screens to large screens.

Bar code

At precisely 8.01 a.m. on 26 June 1974 a packet of Wrigley's chewing gum with a bar code printed on it was passed over the scanner at a checkout in the Marsh Supermarket, Troy, Ohio, and thereby became the first product to be logged using the new computerized recognition system. The bar code first appeared in Britain on a box of Melrose 100 Century tea bags in 1978.

The printed bar code mark which now appears on practically all retail items was invented by IBM and approved for use in 1973. The original version was called the Universal Product Code (UPC) which is the basis of the 12-number American bar code that is now used on almost everything that consumers buy – it is reckoned that some four billion bar codes are scanned every day in the USA and Canada. In Europe, EAN (European Article Number) is a

Detail from **Generic Man** *by Jana Sterbak, 1989. You can't tell the price of a haircut by simply looking at the bar code. You can't see the bar code without eyes in the back of your head.*

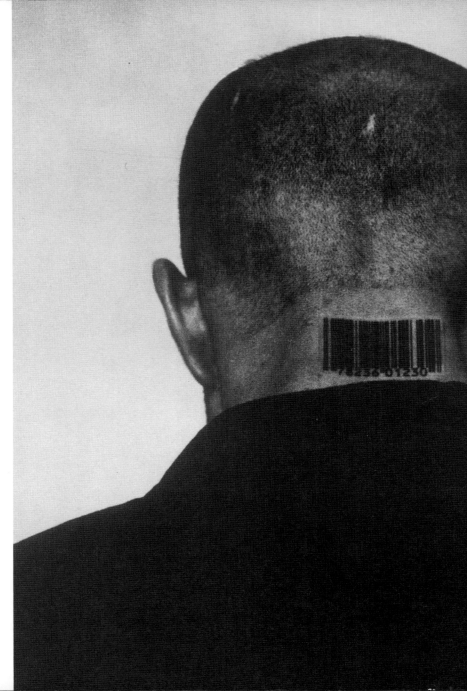

development of the UPC and has 13 numbers. Essential to the working of the bar code system are the electronic point-of-sale machines at checkouts.

The idea has transformed the retail industry, yet it is very simple. The lines of each bar code uniquely represent the manufacturer's identity and an assigned product number. This information is 'read' by scanning it at the checkout with a laser beam that moves at around 10,000 inches per second and transfers it to the retailer's database computer. There it is correlated with the store's own information, which includes the price and a range of other data such as description, size, manufacturer and stock inventory. The database computer then confirms the item back to the checkout where the product description and price are displayed and added to the bill. All this happens in a matter of nanoseconds.

The bar code system is practically error-proof, and in terms of managing and controlling stock has made life much easier for retailers. It helps marketing people by quickly identifying which items are selling and which are not. It has also made checkouts on average 10 per cent faster and gives the shopper a complete itemized receipt. Initially only designers of packaging and book and magazine covers objected to what they regarded as this unwanted graphic intrusion. By the end of the century bar codes are almost universal and nobody seems to notice their presence any more.

J'❤️IME NEW YORK

© 1980 LA LIBRAIRIE DE FRANCE, ROCKEFELLER CENTER, NEW YORK ®

STICKER: SEND $1.00 TO

I ❤️ O

I Love NY

Perhaps the most memorable piece of graphic design to come out of the century was Milton Glaser's rendition of the 'I Love New York' campaign line, which appeared in 1977. Reducing the 'love' to its symbol and 'New York' to its initials he produced a simple and appealing piece of popular code. It spearheaded a campaign conceived by Charlie Hans of the Madison Avenue advertising agency Wells, Rich, Greene and public relations consultant Bobby Zaren, who actually came up with the slogan.

In the mid-1970s New York City was in turmoil: it was bankrupt; its reputation as a place to live or a place to visit was shot. Presiding over the collapse of the city's finances and its self-respect was the dashing Mayor Lindsey. He went cap in hand to Washington for money while police, firefighters and other municipal employees waited for overdue pay cheques. Yet New Yorkers knew that their city was a great deal better than its reputation, and the 1977 'I Love New York' campaign was conceived to tell the world just that. Such was its success that Glaser's graphic device has become one of the most imitated ever.

Designer Milton Glaser said: 'Nothing I have done before or since has had such a tremendous effect. The world must have been waiting for it'. And the world sincerely flattered the logo with numerous imitations.

Post-it Note

In 1981, the 3M Corporation in the USA began marketing pads of small blank notes, characteristically yellow, which had a special kind of glue along one edge. The glue was easily separated, left no residue and was reusable. The neat invention soon caught on and by the end of the century its use in offices and homes was ubiquitous. The countless uses of Post-it Notes range from marking the place in a book to leaving messages on milk bottles.

The invention of the Post-it Note was one of the great research-and-development accidents of all time. Spencer Silver was working as a research chemist on adhesive technology at 3M when in 1970 he came up with a glue that was reluctant to stick to anything for long.

Silver's express mission had been to produce the strongest glue on the market. Having come up with quite the opposite, his reputation seemed shot. Yet he was not downhearted as he noticed that his new glue did have interesting properties. It could be reused, and it left no residue on the material to which it was applied. For ten years he tried to find an application for his glue, but nobody at 3M was interested.

Then a colleague of Silver's, one Arthur Fry, stumbled on the answer. Fry was a singer in his local church choir and would mark his hymn book carefully every Sunday with slips of paper. And every Sunday as he opened his book the slips would fall out. Fry remembered Silver's 'useless' glue and applied it to the slips of paper, which held in place. In 1981, a year after Fry's revelation, 3M started production of the first Post-it Notes. A remarkable little piece of innovation was born. Post-it Notes are now manufactured in all sorts of shapes, colours and sizes as the idea has caught on in homes and offices all around the world.

Builders' chute

The rubbish chute that looks like a stack of plastic dustbins hanging off the scaffolding on building sites was developed and patented in 1984 by G. H. Vlutters and A. J. Vlutters in the Netherlands. Their building equipment company, Vlutters, introduced the first purpose-made rubbish chute system the same year. The idea came from the way plastic cups stack into long white snakes – take out the bottoms and you have a modular bendy tube.

One of the first builders' chutes to be employed was in the restoration of a church in Cologne, when a chute 300 ft (90 m) long was used from the roof. Since then the principle has been adopted for a variety of other purposes. It is used in the Middle East to convey cargo over the sides of large ships to the docks. Submarine cable layers also use the same idea to guide their cables on to the seabed.

Prozac

In 1972 Lilly Industries synthesized fluoxetine, a new kind of anti-depressant drug that came to be called Prozac. It was first introduced to the Belgians in 1986, although not necessarily because they are more prone to depression than anyone else. The Americans got it in 1988, managing to turn what is a little pill into new kind of hero and fad among the status-conscious. The British started taking it in 1989, but it's quite hard to tell whether it has made any difference. By 1997 30 million people worldwide had been treated with Prozac with sales reaching $2.56 billion.

Many of the little things that have changed life in the twentieth century were designed to make it easier. Consequently they have also made it faster, which in turn has made it as difficult in other ways as it was before. The ability to work anywhere at any time has been increased. Greater individual freedom has made people less reliant on others. There is more 'interpersonal' competitiveness. Global communications and greater mobility have begun to blur previously well-defined cultures. This is not all good. For many it challenges personal identity and worth, which produces a measure of stress and a sense of alienation.

The traditional remedies for such problems remain – time, laughter and the community of one's family and friends. But for an increasing number, these are not available any more, and they resort to the 'new grandmothers', the psychotherapist and counsellor who dispense their predetermined wisdom from books, or to the modern-day local priests, the GP and alternative-medicine practitioner who dispense their remedies from bottles.

When stress goes out of control and leads to clinical depression the individual is faced with a serious and frightening condition. There is particular neurotransmitter in the brain called serotonin whose levels affect the regulation of mood, appetite and aggression – too little serotonin means more aggression and depression. Prozac works to increase the levels of serotonin in the brain. In this way it rubs out the symptoms of depression, thus reviving the sense of well being.

Prozac has few side effects, is non-addictive and relatively safe in overdose. It is certainly the best treatment for depression yet devised. But it doesn't solve its causes.

Right: The 18 December 1989 issue of New York *magazine, the first time a pill was used for a cover instead of a person.*

Marilyn Monroe's life ended in tragedy when she died in her Californian home at the age of 36 in 1962. Her career had lit up the lives of millions of movie-goers and star-watchers in the 1950s as she moved from being the archetypal 'dumb blonde' to accomplished comedienne and finally serious film actress. Yet she craved the security and happiness she rarely knew and became increasingly prone to fits of depression. These pictures by Bert Stern for Eros magazine were the last ever taken of her.

"Marilyn was a phenomenon of ... like Niagara Falls and the Grand ... You couldn't talk to it ... It couldn't talk back to ..."

$1.95 • DECEMBER 18, 1989

New York

A New
Wonder Drug for
Depression

BYE-BYE
BLUES

By Fran Schumer

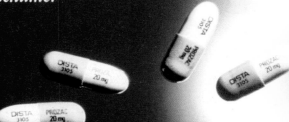

5 1

0 739175

Index

Selected bibliography

Dictionary of Trade Name Origins, Adrian Room, Routledge & Kegan Paul, 1982

The Shell Book of Firsts, Patrick Robertson, Ebury Press & Michael Joseph, 1983

Inventors & Discoverers, Elizabeth L Newhouse, National Geographic Society, 1988

The Fifties, Portrait of a Decade, Peter Lewis, The Herbert Press, 1989

The Packaging Source Book, Robert Opie, MacDonald Orbis, 1989 London

I For Invention, Meredith Hooper, PBK, 1992

They All Laughed, Ira Flatow, Harper Collins, 1992 New York

The Guinness Book of Innovations, Geoff Tibballs, Guinness Publishing, 1994

Encyclopedia of Consumer Brands, Volumes 1-3, St James Press, 1994

Great British Inventions, Mark Tanner, Fourth Estate, 1997

How Household Names Began, Michael O'Mara, 1997 London

Picture credits

Acknowledgements

The authors would especially like to thank the following for their help in the preparation of this book: 3M. Adidas. AHPMA. Alcoa. Anna Baker. The Barbican Library. Lindsey Bareham. BBC Radio. BBC Television. Becton Dickinson. Bic. Birds Eye Walls. Black & Decker. Bristol-Myers. The British Library.

British Steel. British Visqueen. Canon. CIBA-Geigy. CND. Cosmetics, Toiletries, Perfumery Association. Dolmar. Domino Pizza. Dow Chemicals. Du Pont. Electrolux. Eli Lilly. Eylure. Judith Flanders. Pat Ford. Formica. GEC. Henry Gibbs. Gillette. Goblin UK. Granada Television. Hamilton

Beach/Proctor-Silex. Herbert Terry & Sons. Hobart Manufacturing. Hoover & The Hoover Museum. IBM. ICI. The Jerry Springer Show. Johnson & Johnson. King's College London. Kimberley Clark. Myllenda Lay. Loctite. London Rubber Company. London Transport Museum. L'Oréal. L Robinson &

Co. Maclaren. Mars Confectionery. McDonalds. Milton Glaser. Ministry of Transport. Moog. Nestlé. Deborah Osborne. Pharmaceutical Society Library. Philips Lighting. Piaggio. Playtex. Polaroid. Margaret Pope. Procter & Gamble. Rawlplug. Percy Reboul. Remington. Respect for Animals. Reuters. Revlon.

Reynolds Metals Co. Schick Brands. Science Museum. Science Reference & Information Service. Sellotape. Smedley's Foods. Smith & Nephew. Stihl. Tampax. Teleffis Eirann. Tetley. Tetra Pak. Texas Instruments. Thermos. Unilever. United Closures & Plastics. Universal Studios. Vlutters. Volvo.